Storytime Crafts

Kathryn Totten

Alleyside Press

Fort Atkinson, Wisconsin

Published by **Alleyside Press**, an imprint of Highsmith Press
Highsmith Press
W5527 Highway 106
P.O. Box 800
Fort Atkinson, Wisconsin 53538-0800
1-800-558-2110

© Kathryn Totten, 1998
Cover design: Frank Neu

The paper used in this publication meets the minimum requirements of American National Standard for Information Science — Permanence of Paper for Printed Library Material. ANSI/NISO Z39.48-1992.

Library of Congress Cataloging-in-Publication Data
   Totten, Kathryn, 1955-
     Storytime crafts / Kathryn Totten.
       p. cm.
     Includes bibliographical references.
     ISBN 1-57950-023-4 (alk. paper)
     1. Storytelling. 2. Early childhood education--
     Activity programs. I. Title.
     LB1042.T68 1998
     372.67 ' 7--dc21   98-6216
                              CIP

Acknowledgments

The following employees of Arapahoe District have contributed theme ideas, crafts, booklists or games, and have been supportive of the development of this book.

Kathleen Beck, Virginia Brace, Terry Douglas, Val Fetters, Donna Geesaman, Jane Herbel, JoAnn LaGuardia, Carolyn Pickett, Dee Requa, Jean Speight, Julia Thomas.

Thanks to Arapahoe Library District Director, Eloise May, and Public Information Officer, Marlu Burkamp, for administrative support.

Contents

Storytime Themes

Introduction

The purpose of this book is to make it easier to plan creative storytimes that feature simple craft activities. The books that are included in these storytime themes are most suitable for children ages two to six. However, children over age six may enjoy many of the longer stories, especially the multicultural ones.

How to Use This Book

To help you plan your storytime, this book is divided into themed programs. Each storytime theme contains suggestions for books to share, as well as an introductory activity, some rest activities, and a craft. From these you may select the books and activities that appeal to you the most, keeping in mind the audience for whom you are preparing. As you begin to prepare your program, the following reminders will provide a good starting point for creating a program that will be popular and fun to work with. Personalize your storytime by adding rhymes, games and fingerplays that are *your* favorites, and by including new picture books or old favorites you think of as you plan. Telling a story that fits in well with the books you are sharing makes your storytime unique. The next section, Storytelling to Young Children, provides suggestions on how to select and prepare a story to tell. It includes the text of six stories, and lists related to the storytime themes.

Playing to a Young Audience

Experienced storytellers who work with younger children use a number of simple strategies to improve the effectiveness of their programs. After introducing your theme, begin by reading the longest book you have selected. Doing this while the children are fresh, you are more likely to keep their attention for the entire book. After reading a story, allow the children to make comments. Use a rest activity to involve and refocus the children. You are then ready to read a second story. In a 30-minute storytime you may read two or three stories, depending on the length of the books and the number of comments from your audience. Be prepared to delete something you have planned if necessary. The children may want to repeat a rest activity several times if it delights them. You may want to try a rest activity after each story.

The last activity of a storytime should be the craft. You will find that the crafts that appear in this book require a minimum of preparation time, and they are easy for children to complete. There are many good reasons for including crafts with your story programs. Taking a craft home after storytime gives children an opportunity to discuss with their families the books that were read during storytime. The craft may be made as a gift for someone else, or you may suggest that they hang it in their room or on their refrigerator at home. Many children find sitting for stories a bit strenuous, and providing a craft at the end of the storytime may reduce their nervousness. Crafts also strengthen their motor skills and help to prepare them for writing and other school activities.

Storytelling to Young Children

Oral storytelling provides enrichment and entertainment for children of all ages, even the two year olds. It provides them with a good oral communication model as you tell a story in your own words. It exposes them to the variety of inflections in human speech. It increases their ability to listen, follow and imagine as they hear a story being told. It shows them that stories are not confined to books, locked away until they acquire the ability to read. Stories are something that can be remembered and shared even by very young children.

Choosing a Story

Storytelling has been the method for handing down cultural values to the new generation for many centuries. Because of this, there are many folktales to draw upon for your first storytelling experience. The ones printed for you here have been collected and recorded by someone who learned them orally. These stories have been well shaped by years of telling, and will certainly give you a successful start as a storyteller.

When you're choosing a story to tell to a young audience, be very selective. Choose a story that fits as many of the criteria below as possible:

- You can tell it in five minutes or less.
- It has a simple plot and few characters.
- It has a repetitive phrase or tells a cumulative story (It's easier for you to remember and for the children to follow.)
- You like the story. It if is a favorite of yours, it will show in your face and voice, and it will become a favorite of theirs.

Using Visuals

Once you have selected the story you plan to tell, you may decide to use something visual to assist you with your storytelling. When telling to young children this is often a good idea. Place hats or masks on several children and make them the characters in your story. Wear an article of clothing that suggests your character. Place figures on a flannel board or magnet board as you tell the story. Use puppets or toys as your story characters. If your story calls for it, creatively search for just the right visual tools.

Using Your Voice

Use vocal inflection that will define your characters. In "Goldilocks and the Three Bears," the Papa bear speaks with a low, authoritative voice. The Mama bear speaks with a sweet, gentle voice. The Baby Bear speaks nervously and with a high voice. My mother told it that way, didn't yours? Keep regional accents to a minimum, as they are distracting. The use of local slang, or a slight broadening or clipping of a word can be enough to suggest the origin of the character. Use variety in the pace of your speech. *The Little Engine That Could*, by Watty Piper, is a good example. If you are telling this story, when the little engine is climbing the hill saying, "I think I can. I think I can," speak slower and slower as he climbs. Once he is heading downhill the phrase, "I thought I could," should be spoken very rapidly. Thoughtful use of your voice will make your story come alive.

Practice, Practice, Practice

Planning and practice are important. Many elements of good storytelling will come to you naturally if you are comfortable with your story and know it well. If you have heard yourself make the voices a few times, it will not sound strange to you. If you have worked with your visual tools a few times there will be no awkwardness. But by all means, if you feel inspired during the telling of your story to use a posture, voice or phrase you never practiced, accept that gift and use it. A story is different each time it is told, because your audience is different and the weather is different and your mood is different. Always leave a story better than you found it, by adding a bit of your own personality to it.

Prepare Your Audience

The first few times you tell stories in your presentation you may get questions from the children such as, "Aren't you going to read it?" or "Where are the pictures?" It will help them to get ready to hear an oral story if you explain that you are going to tell the story in your own words. You may tell them that the pictures will be very special because they get to make them up in their head. You may even invite them to help you tell the story. Teach them to say a phrase that is repeated often in the story. Give them some actions to do as you tell it.

Creatively involve your audience in the story and you will have a magical experience together.

You can find good stories to tell in many places. You may expand a joke into a good story.

You may tell a story from a magazine. You may remember a story you heard as a child, or relate a personal episode from your childhood. If you begin your search for a story in a collection of folktales, you will have knowledge that these stories have entertained generations of children. A few stories suitable for telling are included in this book. Perhaps one of them will become a favorite for you as you build your storytelling repertoire.

Suggested reading for storytellers

Cole, Joanna. *Best-Loved Folktales of the World.* Doubleday, 1982. Includes stories from Europe, the Middle East, Asia, the Pacific Islands, North and South America. The sources are listed and an index of categories is included.

Dubrovin, Vivian. *Storytelling for the Fun of It: A Handbook for Children.* Storycraft Publishing, 1994. Explains on a child's level how to find and prepare stories to tell for many kinds of events.

Maguire, Jack. *Creative Storytelling: Choosing, Inventing, and Sharing Tales for Children.* McGraw-Hill, 1985. Discusses selecting, creating and presenting stories.

Miller, Teresa and Anne Pelowski, edited by Norma Livo. *Joining In: An Anthology of Audience Participation Stories & How to Tell Them.* Yellow Moon Press, 1988. Stories from various storytellers with notes from them on how they perform the story.

Thompson, Stith. *One Hundred Favorite Folktales.* Indiana University Press, 1968. The collection includes stories from France, Norway, Spain, Italy, Egypt, Germany and other countries and includes notes, sources and tale types.

Stories to Tell...

The Wide-Mouth Frog

Once upon a time there was a lovely little stream. Growing thick along the banks were tall grasses and wild flowers. In a wide spot in the stream there lived a wide-mouthed frog *(open mouth wide every time you say this phrase)*. Mrs. Wide-mouth Frog was going to have a family very soon. But she didn't know what to feed her babies. As all mothers do, she decided to ask some other mothers for advice. Mrs. Wide-mouth Frog went hop, hop, hop down the path until she came to Mrs. Cow.

She said, *(open your mouth very wide when she talks)* "Mrs. Cow, please do tell me, what do you feed your babies?"

Mrs. Cow answered, "I feed them mmmm-milk!"

Mrs. Wide mouth frog did not have any milk to feed her babies, but she politely said, "Oh, thank you very much."

She went down the road again, hop, hop, hop, until she came to Mrs. Dog lying in the sun. She asked, "Mrs. Dog, please do tell me, what do you feed your babies?"

Mrs. Dog looked up at Mrs. Wide-mouth Frog and barked, "Bones! I feed them bones!"

"Oh, thank you very much," said Mrs. Wide-mouth Frog. But she didn't have any bones to feed her babies. She decided to try asking someone who lived in the water as she did. Perhaps the advice would be more useful. So Mrs. Wide-mouth Frog went hop, hop, hop, down to the banks of the stream, where the water is very blue and very deep. There she found Mrs. Alligator nearly hidden in the tall plants near the banks.

"Mrs. Alligator, please do tell me, what do you feed your babies?" asked Mrs. Wide-mouth Frog.

Mrs. Alligator rose up a little in the water. Across her face a smile slowly spread. She came close to the bank and said. "I feed them wide-mouth frogs!"

"Oh. Thank you very much." said Mrs. Wide-mouth Frog *(speak with mouth nearly closed and lips pulled in tightly)*. And she never again opened her mouth wide after that.

Another version can be found in: *Tales for Telling From Around the World* by Mary Medlicott. Kingfisher Books, 1992.

Related story themes: Animal Babies, Frogs, Mothers

Pair this story with another about an animal on a quest such as *The Lion and the Little Red Bird* by Elisa Klevin (See Birds).

Lazy Jack

English Folktale

Once there was a boy who never did any work at all. People called him Lazy Jack. One day his mother said, "It is time to seek your fortune." So Jack went to work for a neighbor. He worked all day, and the neighbor gave him a penny. Jack started home with the penny in his hand, but along the way he dropped it.

"Silly boy," said his mother. "You should have put it in your pocket."

"I will next time," promised Jack. The next day he went to work for a farmer. He worked all day, and the farmer gave him a pitcher of milk. Jack remembered what his mother said. He put the pitcher in his pocket. As he walked along, the milk splashed out of the pitcher. By the time he got home, there was no milk left at all and his clothes were a mess.

"Silly boy," said his mother. "You should have carried it on your head."

"I will next time," promised Jack. The next day he found work with a butter maker. He worked all day, and the man gave him a pound of butter. Jack remembered what his mother said. He put the butter on his head. The sun was very hot, and as Jack walked home, the butter melted down over his ears and face.

"Silly boy," said his mother. "You should have carried it in your hands."

"I will next time," said Jack. The next day he worked for an old woman, who had nothing to give him but a tomcat. Jack picked up the cat and carried it in his hands as he started along the road. The cat didn't like that. He scratched poor Jack so much that he had to let go.

"Silly boy," said his mother. "You should have tied it with a string and led it along behind you."

"I will next time," said Jack. The next day Jack worked for a butcher. He worked all day, and the butcher gave him a leg of lamb. Jack remembered what his mother said. He tied a string to the leg of lamb and pulled it along behind him. By the time Jack got home the leg of lamb was all covered with dirt.

"Silly boy," said his mother. "You should have carried it on your shoulder."

"I will next time," said Jack. The next day Jack worked for a farmer, who gave him a donkey at the end of the day. It was very heavy, but Jack put that donkey on his shoulder. He started off for home. Along the way, he passed a house where a rich man lived with his daughter. The daughter was very beautiful, and she had a pretty smile.

But she had never laughed, not once, in her whole life.

The daughter happened to be looking out the window when Jack walked by, carrying a donkey on his shoulders. He looked so funny that she burst out laughing for the very first time! This made her father so happy that he asked Jack to stay and work for him. It was soon very certain that the farmer's daughter loved Jack very much. The farmer asked Jack to be his daughter's husband. So the two of them were married, and moved into a fine house on the farm. Lazy Jack became rich, and he was no longer lazy. He invited his mother to live with them. She did not tell him how to do his work, and Jack prospered by doing things his own way. They lived happily ever after.

Picture book versions of this story:

Lazy Jack by Tony Ross. Dial, 1986.

Obedient Jack by Paul Galdon. Watts, 1972.

Another version can be found in:

MultiCultural Folktales by Judy Sierra. Oryx, 1991.

Related story themes: Mothers

Pair this with another cumulative story, or with a story about a clever main character. Point out some similarities between the stories. You might use *Dance Away* by George Shannon (see Rabbits) or *The Little Red Ant and the Great Big Crumb* by Shirley Climo (see Ants).

The Gingerbread Man

Traditional Folktale

Once upon a time there lived a little old lady and a little old man. Their home was in a tiny house in a green valley. The little old man liked to work in the garden. He grew all kinds of good things to eat. The little old woman liked to work in her kitchen baking pies, cakes and cookies. One morning she decided to bake something special. The little old lady mixed the dough, and rolled the dough, and cut the dough into a little gingerbread man. "He will keep us company," she said.

The little old lady popped him into the oven to bake. While he baked she sat in her rocking chair and rocked, and rocked, and rocked some more. The house began to smell very good. She opened the oven door just a crack to see if the gingerbread man was baked. He was! He winked at her! Then he hopped out of the oven and ran across the kitchen to the open door.

"Stop! You are supposed to keep us company," cried the little old lady. The gingerbread man ran through the garden. "Stop," cried the little old man. The gingerbread man just laughed and said, "Run, run, as fast as you can. You can't catch me. I'm the gingerbread man." Then he ran through the garden gate and down the road. The little old lady and the little old man ran after him.

The gingerbread man ran past two men cutting wheat in a field. "Stop!" shouted the first man, as he saw the gingerbread man running by. "Stop!" cried the second man. Together they ran after him, but the gingerbread man only laughed and said, "Run, run, as fast as you can. You can't catch me. I'm the gingerbread man. I'm running away from the little old lady and the little old man, and I can run away from you, too. I can!"

Soon the gingerbread man passed a cow in the meadow. "Stop, dooooooo!" cried the cow. But the gingerbread man laughed at the cow and said, "Run, run, as fast as you can. You can't catch me, I'm the gingerbread man. I'm running away from the little old lady and the little old man, and the two men in the field. I can run away from you, too. I can!"

Then the gingerbread man ran past a pink pig soaking in a puddle. "Oink. Stop!" cried the pig. But the gingerbread man laughed and said, "Run, run, as fast as you can. You can't catch me, I'm the gingerbread man. I'm running away from the little old lady and the little old man, the two men in the field and the cow. I can run away from you, too. I can!

At last the gingerbread man came to a river, and he had to stop. Just then a fox peeked out from the bushes. "Hop onto my back," said the fox. "I will carry you across the river." He smiled a large smile, showing all of his shiny, sharp teeth. The gingerbread man climbed on. The fox started swimming. As the water got deeper, water began to cover his back. "Hop onto my nose, gingerbread man," he said. "I don't want you to get wet and soggy." The gingerbread man hopped, but he never landed on the fox's nose. Snap! The fox's shiny teeth closed over him. The fox swallowed him down. At last the little old lady, the little old man, the two men from the field, the cow and the pig came to the edge of the river. They got there just in time to see the fox eat the gingerbread man. After all, that is what gingerbread men are for.

"Oh, well," said the little old lady. "I will just go home and bake another." And she did.

Picture book versions of this story:
The Gingerbread Man by Eric Kimmel. Holiday House, 1993.
The Gingerbread Man by Carol North. Golden, 1988.

Related story themes: Cows, Pigs

This story can add variety to any theme. If you ask the children to run in place each time you say "run, run," it provides them with a physical release for extra energy.

The Never-Ending Bannocks

A Tale from Scotland

There once was an woman, tending to her garden and singing a lovely song. Suddenly there were two little men at her garden gate. "Come quickly," they said. "A new mother needs you."

She agreed to go with them. They took her to a house she had never seen, though she had lived on that hill all her life. As they came in the door, the two men washed their hands and faces in a bowl of water. The woman washed her face and hands, too. They took her to the woman of the house who had a new baby boy. Then one of the little men said, "Bake us some bannocks. The new mother will have need of some food. Just put the scrapings of oatmeal from the board back in the jar. When the jar is empty, we will take you home." The woman agreed to help, and she started baking.

She mixed the meal into batter and baked it in a pan. When the batter was mixed she put the scrapings in the jar. She was sure the jar should be nearly empty, but each time she looked inside it was half full, just as it was when she started.

She mixed and mixed and mixed.
She baked and baked and baked.
She scraped up the meal and put it in the jar.
She mixed and mixed and mixed.
She baked and baked and baked.
She scraped up the meal and put it in the jar.
The poor woman had been baking bannocks all day long, and still the jar was half full. "I just want to go home," she said to herself. "But these are never-ending bannocks."

"You will never be done if you put the spare meal back," said the new mother, who was chewing a warm bannock. "Fling it on the fire." The woman scraped up the meal from the board and flung it on the fire. Poof! The fire burned it up. Soon, all the meal was used up. "They would have kept you here baking forever," said the new mother. "It is good that you listened to me."

So the men came back, and seeing that the meal was gone, they took the woman home. Some while later, she was again working in her garden. She looked across the meadow and saw one of the little men.

"Oh, it's you. How is the mother and the wee boy?" she asked.

"Do you see me?" asked the little man. "With which eye?"

"With both," said the woman.

"Did you wash with our water?" asked the little man.

"Oh, yes," she said, "Just as you did when you went into the house."

"We will soon fix that," said the little man. He came right up to her face, and blew a kiss in her eyes. Instantly the little man vanished, and she never saw the fairies again.

Related story themes: Mothers

Pair this story with another story about food, or with a fairy tale from France, Ireland or Germany. You might use *The Wolf's Chicken Stew* by Keiko Kasza (see Chickens).

The Snake

Once a possum was walking through the woods, and he came to a deep hole in the middle of the road. Possum stopped, and scratched his head. "I don't remember seeing that hole before," he said to himself. Then he heard a tiny, pitiful voice calling to him.

"Help me, possum. Help me."

Possum looked into the hole, because that is where the voice was coming from. There in the bottom he saw a snake! He heard it call again, "Help me, possum. Help me."

"What's the matter?" called Possum, from a safe distance.

"I've been down in this hole a long time," said the snake. "And I have a brick on my back. Won't you come down here and lift it off for me?"

"Oh, no," said Possum. "I know you. If I get down there you will bite me!"

"Maybe not," said the snake. "Maybe not. Maybe not."

Well Possum was good hearted, and he couldn't just walk away with that snake in such a predicament, so he started thinking. He thought high, and he thought low. While he was thinking high, he saw a dead branch on a tree overhead. Possum broke it off, and reached down into the hole with it. He pushed that brick off of the snake's back. Feeling better about it, he walked away. He didn't get past the first bend in the road before he heard it again.

"Help me, Possum. Oh, help me."

Even though he wanted to keep going, Possum stopped, because he couldn't just leave a creature in trouble. "What is it now," asked Possum.

"I've been down in this hole a long time," said the snake in a pitiful, whiney voice. "I can't get out by myself. Won't you come down and lift me up?"

"Oh, no," said Possum. "I know you. If I get down in that hole you will bite me!"

"Maybe not," said the snake. "Maybe not. Maybe not."

"OK," said Possum finally. "I will help you, but I'm staying away from you!" Possum used that same branch that he used before. He scooted it under the snake's belly, and flung him into the air. Snake soared up over the trees and landed somewhere in the dark forest.

Possum felt better and started down the road. He didn't get past the second bend in the road before he heard it again.

"Help me, Possum. Oh, help me."

"Where are you," called Possum, "and what do you want now?"

"Possum, I was in that hole such a long, long time. Now I'm cold and stiff. I can't even move my tail. Won't you pick me up and put me in your pocket, just for awhile? Just until I get warm?"

"Oh, no," said Possum. "If I pick you up and put you in my pocket, you will bite me."

"Maybe not," said the snake. "Maybe not. Maybe not."

"Oh, all right," said Possum. He just could not leave another creature suffering so. He walked into the dark forest, stepping carefully so he would not squash the snake. When he found him, he carefully coiled the snake up and put him in his pocket. Possum continued down the road, and soon forgot all about the snake. By about the third bend in the road the snake was warm. Slowly he uncoiled himself, and began to climb up Possum's body. He curled around Possum's arm. He slithered up Possum's neck, and stared into Possum's face.

"Oh, it's you," said Possum. "I forgot I was carrying you with me."

"Now," said snake, "I suppose I will bite you."

"What? You are going to bite me? After everything I did for you?" Possum cried. "What kind of a thank you is that?"

"Oh, don't look so surprised," said the snake. "You knew I was a snake when you picked me up."

Another version of this story can be found in:
"Brer Possum's Dilemma," told by Jackie Torrence in *Homespun Tales from America's Favorite Storytellers.* Jimmy Neil Smith. Crown, 1988.

Related story themes: Snakes

Pair this story with another story about a possum such as *Possum Magic* by Mem Fox (see Australia).

Africa

Before Sharing Books

Hang artificial vines from the doorway of your storytime area. As the children assemble, tell them you are going to the jungle in Africa. Ask them what kind of animals they expect to see there. Accept all suggestions, then tell them you will show them pictures of some African animals in the books you have selected. Tell them to look for the animal they suggested in the books. Then walk through the vines and enjoy your safari!

Rest Activities

Fingerplays and Action Rhymes

Here Comes the Elephant

Here comes the elephant,
Crash, crash, crash. *(stomp feet)*
Here comes the cheetah,
Dash, dash, dash. *(run quickly in place)*
Here comes the monkey,
Swing, swing, swing. *(arms over head)*
Here comes the lion,
He's the king. Roar! *(walk proudly and roar)*

The Gorilla

This is the way the gorilla walks. *(crouch down, let arms hand long)*
This is the way the gorilla eats. *(chew leaves)*
This is the way the gorilla talks,
Ooh, ooh, ooh!
This is the way the gorilla sleeps. *(head on hands and snore loudly)*

Game

Drums Are Calling!

Clap a rhythm for the children to repeat.
Vary the rhythm several times.

Books to Share

Alderman, Dan. *Africa Calling: Nightime Falling.* Whispering Coyote Press, 1996. A girl imagines herself in Africa with lions, elephants, monkeys, rhinos, zebras and other animals.

Deetlefs, Rene. *Tabu and the Dancing Elephants.* Dutton, 1995. A young boy named Tabu is taken away by an old mama elephant while his father is asleep. Tabu's mother gets him back by teaching the elephants how to dance.

Diakite, Baba Wague. *The Hunterman and the Crocodile.* Scholastic, 1997. Donso, a West African hunterman, learns the importance of living in harmony with nature and the necessity of placing humans among and not above other living creatures.

Gerson, Mary-Joan. *Why the Sky Is Far Away: A Folktale From Nigeria.* Little, Brown, 1992. The sky was once so close to Earth that people cut parts of it to eat, but their waste and greed caused the sky to move far away.

Kimmel, Eric. *Anansi and the Talking Melon.* Holiday House, 1994. A clever spider tricks Elephant and some other animals into thinking the melon in which he is hiding can talk.

Mollel, Tololwa. *Ananse's Feast: An Ashanti Tale.* Clarion, 1997. Unwilling to share his feast, Ananse the spider tricks Akye the turtle so that he can eat all the food himself, but Akye finds a way to get even.

Mwenye, Hadithi. *Greedy Zebra.* Little, Brown, 1984. This story tells how the animals of the world acquired their colorful furs and spots and how Zebra's greedy appetite caused him to get stripes.

Rosen, Michael. *How Giraffe Got Such a Long Neck - And Why Rhino Is So Grumpy.* Dial, 1993. During a terrible drought, Man prepares a magic herb that results in Giraffe's long neck so he can reach the leaves on trees. Rhino is grumpy because he arrives too late for the magic.

Beaded Bracelet

Zimbabwe and the Republic of South Africa are famous for glass beaded bracelets. Here are two methods for making them.

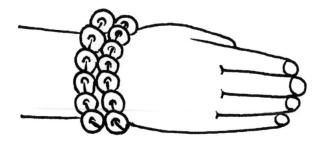

Directions

For each child, cut a piece of strong string 12" long. Wrap a piece of tape tightly around one end to make it stiff enough for stringing. For children under age six, use colorful ring cereal for beads. Slide on one ring and tie it in place. Allow the children to complete the string, then tie it around their wrist.

For children over age six, craft beads can be used. Select a variety of wooden, glass or plastic beads with a large hole. Slide one bead on the string and tie it in place. Allow the children to complete the string, then tie it around their wrist. If time permits, they may make two strings of beads and tie them together for a double bracelet.

This craft takes **10 minutes** to complete.

Animal Babies

Before Sharing Books

This storytime works well in the spring. If possible, have community members bring baby lambs, chicks, puppies or piglets to show.

Rest Activities

Fingerplays and Action Rhymes

Five Little Ducks

Five little ducks went out to play, *(hold up five fingers)*
Over the hills and far away, *(make a hill with hand and point away)*
The mother duck said,
"Quack, quack, quack." *(make hands talk like a duck bill)*
Four little ducks came running back. *(run in place)*
Count down to one.

This Little Pig

This little pig went to market. *(wiggle big toe)*
This little pig went home. *(wiggle second toe)*
This little pig had roast beef. *(wiggle third toe)*
This little pig had none. *(wiggle fourth toe)*
This little pig cried, "Wee, wee, wee." *(wiggle little toe)*
All the way home.

Songs

Baby Bumble Bee

Oh, I'm bringing home a baby bumble bee.
Won't my mother be so proud of me?
Oh, I'm bringing home a baby bumble bee.
Ouch! He stung me.

Mary Had a Little Lamb

Mary had a little lamb, little lamb, little lamb.
Mary had a little lamb with fleece as white as snow.

*Complete version in: **Mary Had a Little Lamb** by Sarah J. Hale. Orchard Books, 1995.*

Books to Share

Barber, Antonia. *Gemma and the Baby Chick.* Scholastic, 1993. Gemma, who collects eggs from the hen house, discovers a hen sitting on her eggs and helps save a chick that is slow to hatch.

Baron, Alan. *Red Fox and the Baby Bunnies.* Candlewick, 1997. Red Fox is out hunting for his supper. He sees the baby bunnies and says, "Yum, yum, yum." Luckily Dan Dog and Tabby Cat are nearby and come to the rescue.

Hoban, Tana. *Who Are They?* Greenwillow, 1994. Black silhouettes against white background depict different mother animals and their young, from one sheep to five ducks.

Moore, Elaine. *Roly-Poly Puppies: A Counting Book.* Scholastic, 1996. Rhyming text and illustrations introduce the numbers one through ten as an ever-growing group of puppies play outdoors.

Rylant, Cynthia. *Everyday Pets.* Bradbury, 1993. The bunnies, ducks, dogs and other everyday pets enjoy sleeping in the sun, eating, and making noise.

Scamell, Ragnhild. *Solo Plus One.* Little, Brown, 1992. A tomcat learns a bit about parenting when a baby duck, mistaking him for its mother, begins to follow him everywhere.

Tafuri, Nancy. *Have You Seen My Duckling?* Greenwillow, 1984. A mother duck leads her brood around the pond as she searches for one missing duckling.

Little Lamb

After your stories, help the children make a little lamb.

Directions

Copy the lamb on white construction paper and cut out one per child. Let the children glue cotton balls on the lamb to make it fluffy. Use markers to draw on a face. Use washable white glue and spread newspapers on the table to make cleanup easier.

 This craft takes **10 minutes** to complete.

Ants

Before Sharing Books

Lead the children on an imaginary adventure, using real or pantomimed picnic materials. "Let's pretend we're on a picnic. What shall we have to eat? I'll look in this picnic basket. Here are some grapes. Here is fried chicken. Here is some bread. There is a cherry pie in this basket, too. What a nice picnic, but I think there is more food than we can eat. Who shall we invite to eat with us? I know. I'm thinking of someone very small, with long legs who likes picnics a lot. Usually they come to picnics in large groups. Do you know who I'm thinking of?"

Rest Activities

Fingerplays and Action Rhymes

Let's Have a Picnic

Let's have a picnic. (rub tummy)
I'll bring the cake. (point to self)
You bring the sandwiches. (point away)
The best you can make. (clap once)
After we eat, we'll play and dance. (hold hands
  with neighbor and dance around)
Picnic is over! Here come the ants! (run away)

If I Were an Ant

If I were an ant, I'd spend an hour,
Climbing up a lovely flower. (hand over hand,
  reaching high)
If I were an ant, I'd go for a ride,
On the back of dog with a long, long stride. (take
  three giant steps)
If I were an ant, I'd look for a tree,
And climb to the top, where I could see. (hand on
  forehead, look far away)
If I were an ant, I'd follow you home,
And hide by your table to wait for crumbs. (rub
  tummy, say, "Yum!")

Song

The Ants Go Marching

Tune of: "When Johnny Comes Marching Home"
The ants go marching one by one,
Hurrah! Hurrah!
The ants go marching one by one,
Hurrah! Hurrah!
The ants go marching one by one,
The little one stops to suck his thumb,
And we all go marching down,
to the ground, to get out of the rain.
Boom, boom, boom.

The ants go marching two by two, etc.
The little one stops to tie his shoe, etc.
The ants go marching three by three, etc.
The little one stops to climb a tree, etc.
[Traditional song]

Another version can be found in: *The Ants Go Marching* by Bernice Freschet. Scribner, 1973.

[handwritten note:] IF I were an ant
ER Moses

Books to Share

Allinson, Beverly. *Effie.* Scholastic, 1990. When Effie the ant's loud voice saves the day, the other insects learn to appreciate her unique gift.

Climo, Shirley. *The Little Red Ant and the Great Big Crumb: A Mexican Fable.* Clarion, 1995. A small red ant finds a crumb in a Mexican corn field, but she thinks she is too small to carry it, so she searches for someone who can.

Grossman, Bill. *My Little Sister Ate One Hare.* Crown, 1996. Little sister eats one hare, two snakes, and three ants, but watch out when she gets to ten peas.

Pince[...] [...] *[...]Ants.* Houg[...] [...] hungry ants head [...] [...] r their tummies.

Van [...] [...]oughton Mifflin, 1988. When two bad ants desert from their colony, they experience a dangerous adventure that convinces them to return to their former safety.

Wolkstein, Diane. *Step By Step.* Morrow, 1994. A little ant and her friend enjoy a day together, dining on the nectar of a yellow flower, sailing on a leaf, and dancing in the rain.

Dancing Ants

After your stories help the children make dancing ants. These are the best kind of ants to take to a picnic.

Directions
Copy the pattern for each child. Cut out. Let the children color their ants. Glue a craft stick to the back of each ant to make stick puppets. Allow time to make the puppets dance.

 This craft takes 5 minutes to complete.

Apples

Before Sharing Books

Tell the children that once a man named Johnny walked across the country planting apple seeds everywhere he went. People called him Johnny Appleseed. The apple seeds grew into big apple trees. Now tell children, "Let's pretend that we are very small apple seeds. Everyone squat down low. Now the rain comes down, and the sun comes out, and we begin to grow. We are getting very tall! Everyone reach their arms up as high as they can. Now we can sit in the shade of the tall apple trees for our stories."

Rest Activities

Fingerplays and Action Rhymes

Up in the Apple Tree

Way up in the apple tree, *(reach arms up high)*
Two little apples were looking at me. *(thumbs and index fingers touch, and circle eyes)*
So I shook and shook and shook that tree, *(shaking motion three times)*
'Til all those apples came down to me. *(bring arms from high to low)*
Mmmmmm. Good! *(pretend to bite the apple)*
[Traditional]

Game

Spooning for Apples

Float apples in a tub of water. Let children take turns trying to scoop one up with a spoon. You may want to have some towels and aprons handy, as this can be a wet game.

Song

I Like Apples
Tune of: "Frere Jacques"
I like apples, I like apples.
Nice and sweet. Nice and sweet.
Crunchy, crunchy, crunchy.
Munchy, munchy, munchy.
Good to eat. Good to eat.
[Adapted traditional song]

Books to Share

Butler, Stephen. *The Mouse and the Apple.* Tambourine, 1994. Other animals come and go while Mouse waits patiently for a ripe apple to fall from a tree.

Charles, Niki N. *What Am I? Looking Through Shapes at Apples and Grapes.* Blue Sky, 1994. Illustrations with cutout shapes and rhyming questions introduce fruits, colors, and shapes.

Dragonwagon, Crescent. *Alligators Arrive With Apples: A Potluck Alphabet Feast.* Macmillan, 1987. Foods are collected for Thanksgiving Day.

Maestro, Betsy. *How Do Apples Grow?* HarperCollins, 1992. Describes the life cycle of an apple from a spring bud to a fully ripe fruit.

Orbach, Ruth. *Apple Pigs.* Collins & World, 1977. A family suddenly has many apples from their old apple tree and finds creative ways to use them.

Priceman, Marjorie. *How to Make an Apple Pie and See the World.* Random House, 1994. Since the market is closed, the reader is led around the world to gather the ingredients for making an apple pie.

Rockwell, Anne. *Apples and Pumpkins.* Collier Macmillan, 1989. In preparation for Halloween night, a family visits Mr. Comstock's farm to pick apples and pumpkins.

Apple Critters

This storytime works very well in the fall, when apples are plentiful. Finish your storytime by allowing the children to create apple critters. Since sharp toothpicks will be used, adult help for each child is recommended. An alternate method is included, if you prefer to make paper apple critters.

Apple Critter

Apple Pattern

Paper Apple Critter

Directions for Apple Critter
Provide an apple for each child. Using toothpicks or plastic hors d'oeuvre picks, attach facial features to the apples. You may use raisins, sliced carrots, cut green peppers, green grapes, cereal, mini marshmallows or any other small foods as facial features.

Alternate Directions for Paper Apple Critter
Cut out an apple shape from red paper for each child, using the pattern here. Cut out small squares and triangles from colored paper. Allow the children to create faces using the small pieces of colored paper. Let them glue faces on the apple shape.

 This craft takes **10 minutes** to complete.

Australia

Before Sharing Books

Tell the children you are going on a bus ride in a far away place. Point and say "Look! I see kangaroos." Everyone hops like a kangaroo. Say, "Look! Now I see crocodiles in the water." Everyone crawls like crocodiles. "Now I see quiet, cuddly koalas in the tree." Everyone settles down and gets cuddly. Ask the children "Can anyone guess what far away place we have come to?"

Rest Activities

Fingerplays and Action Rhymes

Here Is Australia

Here's the emu straight and tall,
Nodding his head above us all. *(raise one arm, fingers down for the head)*

Here's the long snake on the ground,
Wriggling upon the stone he found. *(wiggle hand and arm)*

Here's the echidna prickly and small,
Rolling himself into a ball. *(curl body and squat)*

Here's the kangaroo jumping around,
Covering yards with every bound. *(jump)*

Here is Australia far away,
That's where our stories come from today.
[Author unknown]

Jump, Jump, Kangaroo Brown

Jump, jump, Kangaroo brown.
Jump, jump, into town.
Jump, jump, uphill and down.
Jump, jump, Kangaroo brown.
Jump while saying the rhyme.
[Traditional]

Song

The Kookaburra

Kookaburra sits in the old gum tree,
Merry, merry king of the bush is he.
Laugh kookaburra.
Laugh kookaburra.
Gay your life must be.
[Traditional]

Books to Share

Adams, Jeanie. *Going for Oysters.* Whitman, 1994. An Australian Aborigine family spends the weekend fishing and looking for oysters, almost forgetting their grandfather's warning about the swamp.

Baker, Jeannie. *Where the Forest Meets the Sea.* Greenwillow, 1987. On a camping trip in an Australian rain forest with his father, a young boy studies the plants and animals around him and wonders about the future.

Cox, David. *Bossyboots.* Crown, 1987. Bossy Abigail infuriates her stagecoach companions on the Australian frontier, but when the coach is held up by outlaws her bossiness comes in handy.

Fox, Mem. *Possum Magic.* Harcourt Brace Jovanovich, 1990. When Grandma Poss's magic turns Hush invisible, the two possums travel all over Australia to find the food that will make her visible again.

Trinca, Rod. *One Wooly Wombat.* Kane/Miller, 1985. Humorous illustrations depict fourteen Australian animals, introduced in rhyme, along with the numbers from one to fourteen.

Vaughan, Marcia K. *Snap!* Scholastic, 1996. Joey the kangaroo plays games with Twister the bush mouse, Slider the snake, Flatso the platypus and other animals. Also: *Wombat Stew*

Winch, John. *The Old Woman Who Loved to Read.* Holiday House, 1997. An old woman moves to the country in order to have a peaceful life with lots of time to read, but soon finds that each season brings others tasks to keep her busy.

Jumping Joey

Bring your journey to Australia to an end by helping the children make a Jumping Joey toy. This craft takes five minutes to complete if all parts are cut and assembled before storytime.

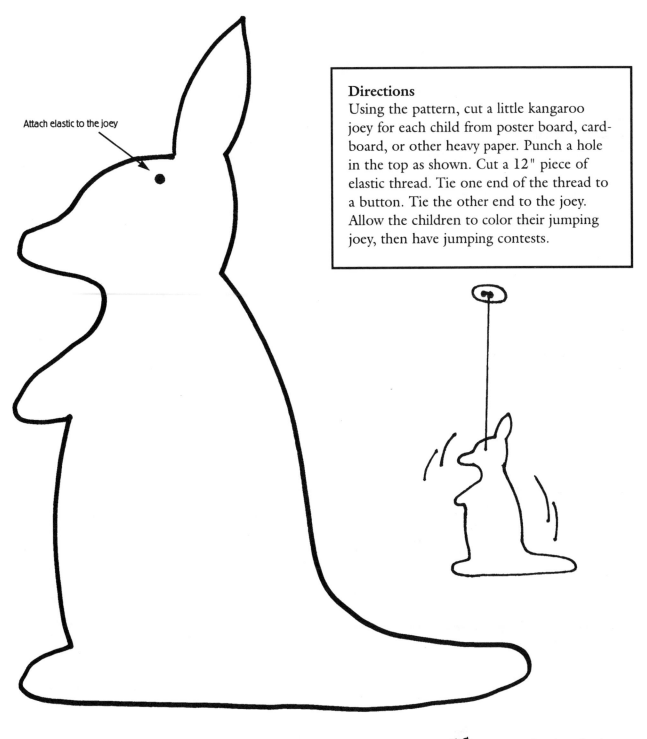

Attach elastic to the joey

Directions
Using the pattern, cut a little kangaroo joey for each child from poster board, cardboard, or other heavy paper. Punch a hole in the top as shown. Cut a 12" piece of elastic thread. Tie one end of the thread to a button. Tie the other end to the joey. Allow the children to color their jumping joey, then have jumping contests.

This craft takes **5 minutes** to complete.

Autumn

Before Sharing Books

Decorate your storytime room with pumpkins, gourds, apples, corn and colorful leaves. Ask the children to raise their hands when you mention their favorite part of this season. List some of your favorites, such as: rain, cool nights, garden vegetables, decorating pumpkins, the sound of geese flying south, walking on crunchy leaves. You may serve popcorn and apple cider at the end of this storytime.

Rest Activities

Fingerplays and Action Rhymes

Popcorn!

Let's make some popcorn nice and hot.

We need a big, round pan. *(make a circle, squat down)*

Pour in a little oil, hear it sizzle. *(say sssssssss)*

Now shake, shake, shake the pan. *(shake whole body)*

Wait a minute, maybe two,

Then you know what the popcorn will do.

Pop! Pop! Pop! Pop! *(as you point to each child in turn, have the child jump up)*

Two Little Blackbirds

Two little blackbirds sitting on a hill, *(hold up index fingers)*

One named Jack, the other named Jill. *(wiggle each index finger)*

Fly away Jack. Fly away Jill. *(put hands behind back one at a time)*

Come back Jack. Come back Jill. *(bring hands to the front again)*

[Traditional rhyme]

Talk about the birds flying away in the fall, but coming back every spring.

Song

Yellow Leaves

Tune of: "London Bridge"

Yellow leaves are falling down,

falling down, falling down.

Yellow leaves are falling down,

Leaves are falling. *(substitute orange, red, brown)*

[Adapted traditional song]

Books to Share

Arnosky, Jim. *Every Autumn Comes the Bear.* Putnam, 1993. Every autumn a bear shows up behind the farm, and goes through a series of routines before finding a den among the hilltop boulders where he sleeps all winter long.

Carlstrom, Nancy White. *Goodbye, Geese.* Philomel, 1991. A father describes the coming of winter to his little girl.

Gersein, Moricai. *Daisy's Garden.* Hyperion, 1995. A young girl and all the animals of the field come together to plant and harvest a garden.

Griffith, Helen. *Alex Remembers.* Greenwillow, 1983. A dog and cat are restless in the autumn moonlight as ancient fears about the season stir in them, but their young owner is there to comfort them.

Laser, Michael. *The Rain.* Simon & Schuster, 1997. In the city, the town, and the forest, people enjoy the beauty of a gentle autumn rainfall.

Moore, Elaine. *Grandma's Smile.* Lothrop, Lee & Shepard, 1995. Kim's grandmother's smile is the inspiration for the jack-o'-lantern face she draws on her pumpkin at a fall festival.

Tresselt, Alvin. *Autumn Harvest.* Mulberry, 1990. Autumn brings the first frost, migrating geese, burning leaves and a fine harvest.

Yolen, Jane. *Beneath the Ghost Moon.* Little, Brown, 1994. Beneath the midnight moon, mice battle mean-hearted creepy crawlies to protect their farmyard home.

Leaf Place Mat

Help the children make a fall place mat. You may use it for your snack of popcorn and apple cider, or just let them take it home to use.

Directions

Gather a large bowl of dry leaves. Cover the work tables with newspaper to protect against crayon marks. Give each child a 12" x 18" sheet of construction paper. Let the children place a few leaves under the paper. Using the side of a crayon, rub the paper until the leaf impressions show through.

 This craft takes 10 minutes to complete.

Bears

Before Sharing Books

You may ask the children to bring their favorite teddy bear from home for this storytime. You may take a few minutes to show and tell the bears. If you bring a bear that you have had since you were young, it will be a hit! You may wish to spread out a blanket on the floor so you can have a teddy bear picnic.

Rest Activities

Fingerplays and Action Rhymes

Ten Bears in the Bed

Ten bears in the bed *(hold up ten fingers)*
And the little one said,
"I'm crowded. Roll over." *(stretch hands out, roll hands)*
So they all rolled over and one fell out! *(hold up nine fingers)*

Continue until there is only one bear left.

Then the little one said, "*I'm lonely!*"

Songs

Teddy Bear, Teddy Bear

Teddy Bear, Teddy Bear, turn around.
Teddy Bear, Teddy Bear, touch the ground.
Teddy Bear, Teddy Bear, show your shoe.
Teddy Bear, Teddy Bear, that will do.
Teddy Bear, Teddy Bear, go upstairs.
Teddy Bear, Teddy Bear, say your prayers.
Teddy Bear, Teddy Bear, turn out the light.
Teddy Bear, Teddy Bear, say good night.
[Traditional song]

The Bear Went Over the Mountain

The bear went over the mountain,
The bear went over the mountain,
The bear went over the mountain,
To see what he could see.

And all that he could see,
And all that he could see,
Was the other side of the mountain,
The other side of the mountain,
The other side of the mountain,
Was all that he could see.
[Traditional song]

Books to Share

Asch, Frank. *Bear Shadow*. Prentice-Hall, 1984. Bear tries everything he can think of to get rid of his shadow.

Barton, Byron. *The Three Bears*. HarperCollins, 1991. This retelling of the Goldilocks adventure has simple, colorful illustrations.

Degen, Bruce. *Jamberry*. Harper & Row, 1983. A little boy walking in the forest meets a big, loveable bear that takes him on a delicious berry-picking adventure.

Dunbar, Joyce. *A Cake for Barney*. Orchard, 1987. When bullies try to take his property, a young bear learns how to stand up to them in a nonviolent way.

Jonas, Anne. *Two Bear Cubs*. Greenwillow Books, 1982. Two adventurous cubs love to wander, but when frightened, appreciate having Mother close by.

Maris, Ron. *Are You There Bear?* Greenwillow Books, 1984. In a darkened room, several toys search for a bear, finally finding him reading a book in a chair.

Young, Ruth. *Golden Bear*. Viking, 1992. Golden Bear and his human companion learn to play the violin, talk to a ladybug, make mudpies and wish on stars.

Bear Treat Cup

Finish up your teddy bear picnic by making a treat cup. This craft takes five minutes if the bears are precut. Allow additional time for eating treats.

Directions

Copy the bear pattern and cut out before storytime. Let children color the bears. Glue a paper cup to the front of the bear, curving his arms around it. A stapler may be used instead, and this will be quicker. Fill the cup with marshmallows, crackers and other treats. Be sure to let parents know a week ahead that treats will be served so they can make other arrangements if their child has allergies.

 This craft takes 5 minutes to complete.

Birds

Before Sharing Books

Collect pictures or toys of many kinds of birds, such as penguins, chickens, parrots, sparrows, turkeys, robins and owls. Ask the children, What is the same about these? (*wings, two legs, feathers, beak*) What is different? (*size, colors, webbed feet, large eyes, small eyes*)

Rest Activities

Fingerplays and Action Rhymes

Two Little Blackbirds

Two little blackbirds sitting on a hill, (*hold up index fingers*)

One named Jack, the other named Jill. (*wiggle each index finger*)

Fly away, Jack. Fly away, Jill. (*put hands behind back one at a time*)

Come back, Jack. Come back, Jill. (*bring hands to the front again*)

[Traditional rhyme]

Dirty Birds

Thirty dirty birds, (*stand up and move hands like beaks*)

Sitting on the curb, (*squat down and move hands like beaks*)

A chirpin',

And a burpin',

And eatin' dirty worms. (*pretend to eat a worm*)

[Traditional rhyme]

Bird Sounds

Big-eyed owl looks all around. (*circle eyes with fingers and turn head left and right*)

Tiny sparrows sit on the ground. (*squat down low*)

Ducks wiggle-waggle as they walk. (*walk like a duck*)

Chickens scratch the ground and squawk. (*slide feet, walk like a chicken*)

Ostriches are very tall. (*reach hands high above head*)

Humming birds are very small. (*hold index finger and thumb close together*)

"Peep, squawk, cheep and whoo" you heard, (*move hands like beak while making the sounds*)

All of those are sounds of birds.

Books to Share

Ardema, Verna. *How the Ostrich Got Its Long Neck.* Scholastic, 1995. A tale from the Akamba people of Kenya that explains why the ostrich has such a long neck.

DePaola, Tomie. ***Days of the Blackbird: A Tale of Northern Italy.*** Putnam, 1997. A pure white bird braves the bitter winter of the northern Italian mountains to sing for a gravely ill man.

Fox, Mem. ***Feathers and Fools.*** Harcourt Brace, 1996. A modern fable about some peacocks and swans who allow fear about their differences to become so great that they end up destroying each other.

Klevin, Elisa. ***The Lion and the Little Red Bird.*** Dutton, 1992. A little bird discovers why the lion's tail changes colors every day.

McLerran, Alice. ***The Mountain That Loved a Bird.*** Picture Book Studio, 1985. A barren mountain becomes an inviting home for the bird it loves.

Maddern, Eric. ***Rainbow Bird: An Aboriginal Folktale from Northern Australia.*** Little, Brown, 1993. When Crocodile Man declares he is "the boss of fire," Rainbow Bird tricks him into sharing it.

Pirotta, Saviour. ***Little Bird.*** Tambourine, 1992. Several animals suggest activities for a little bird who asks, "What can I do today?"

Rosen, Michael. ***Crow and Hawk: A Traditional Pueblo Indian Story.*** Harcourt Brace, 1995. When Crow flies away from her nest, Hawk cares for the eggs. After they hatch, Crow wants her babies back.

Bird

After your birds stories help the children make a little bird to take home.

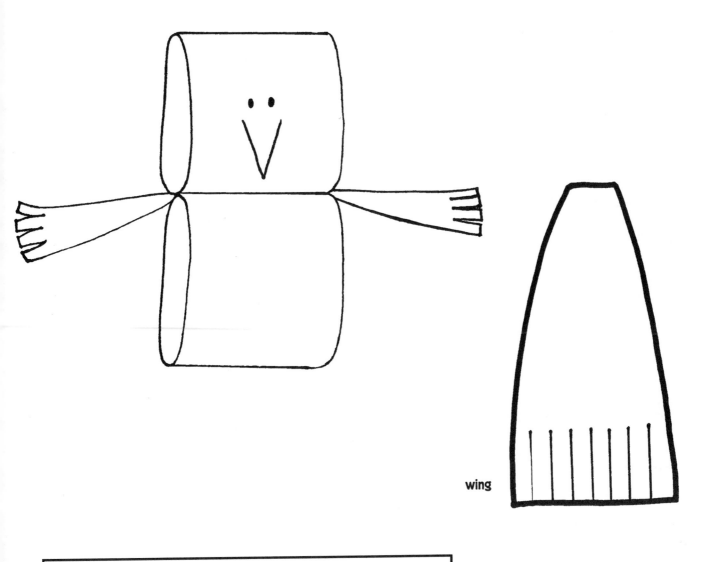

wing

Directions

Cut two paper strips, 8½" X 2" for each child. Using the pattern here, cut a pair of wings for each child. Let child glue the ends of paper strips together, forming two rings. Let child glue the wings as shown between the rings. Let child glue the rings together, forming a figure eight (8). Face can be drawn with markers.

 This craft takes 10 minutes to complete.

Boats

Before Sharing Books

Play a tape of ocean sounds, or boat-related sea-faring music as the children come into the room. Decorate the room with real items if possible, such as nets, ropes, life preservers, a raft or canoe. Rope off an area that will be your storytime boat and seat the children in it. Tell them to pretend they are floating out on the water as you read the stories.

Rest Activities

Fingerplays and Actions Rhymes

Motor Boat, Motor Boat

Motor boat, motor boat, go so slow. *(stamp feet slowly)*

Motor boat, motor boat, go so fast. *(stamp feet faster)*

Motor boat, motor boat, step on the gas! *(stamp feet very fast)*

[Traditional]

Rub a Dub Dub

Rub a dub dub. Three men in a tub.
And who do you think they be?
The butcher, the baker, the candlestick maker,
All rowing their way out to sea.

[Traditional nursery rhyme]

Songs

Row, Row, Row Your Boat

Row, row, row your boat,
Gently down the stream.
Merrily, merrily, merrily, merrily,
Life is but a dream.

[Traditional song]

Michael Row the Boat Ashore

Michael row the boat ashore. Alleluia.
Michael row the boat ashore. Alleluia.

Sister helped to trim the sail. Alleluia.
Sister helped to trim the sail. Alleluia.

[Traditional song]

Books to Share

Ginsburg, Mira. *Four Brave Sailors*. Greenwillow, 1987. Four mice are brave sailors who fear nothing except the cat.

Lear, Edward. *The Owl and the Pussycat*. Illustrated by Jan Brett. Putnam, 1991. After a courtship voyage of a year and a day, Owl and Pussycat buy a ring from Piggy and get married.

Ludwig, Warren. *Old Noah's Elephants*. Putnam, 1991. When two elephants misbehave on Noah's ark, endangering the other animals, God tells Noah that the solution is to tickle the hyena.

McCarthy, Bobbette. *Dreaming*. Candlewick, 1994. Asleep in his cozy bed, a dog dreams of a midnight row out to sea.

Shaw, Nancy. *Sheep in a Ship*. Houghton Mifflin, 1988. Sheep on a deep-sea voyage run into trouble when storms develop and are glad to come paddling into port.

Titherington, Jeanne. *Baby's Boat*. Greenwillow, 1992. A baby falls asleep, and dreams of sailing out in a silver moon boat.

Walnut Boat

After your voyage help the children make and sail a walnut shell boat. Have a tub, wading pool, or sink filled with water so you can float them. This craft takes five minutes to complete. Allow time for boat races!

Directions
Break walnuts, saving shell halves that are intact. Cut sails and ducks from construction paper. Glue them on toothpicks. This should be done before storytime. To assemble the boat, let the children put a small amount of clay in the walnut shell. Insert the sail in the clay. Float the boat. If it is too heavy, remove some of the clay.

This craft takes 5 minutes to complete.

Bugs

Before Sharing Books

If it's the right season to do so, capture a ladybug or other bug. Put it in a bug carrier or a jar with a nylon mesh cover. Show it to the children and ask them to pretend they are very small, like a bug. Have them crawl to a safe place where they can sit and hear the stories.

Rest Activities

Fingerplays and Action Rhymes

Little Miss Muffet
Little Miss Muffet sat on her tuffet,
Eating her curds and whey.
Along came a spider and sat down beside her,
And frightened Miss Muffet away!
[Traditional Rhyme]

Songs

Shoo Fly
Shoo fly, don't bother me,
Shoo fly, don't bother me,
Shoo fly, don't bother me,
For I belong to somebody.

I feel, I feel, I feel,
I feel like the morning star.
I feel, I feel, I feel,
I feel like the morning star.

Shoo fly, don't bother me,
Shoo fly, don't bother me,
Shoo fly, don't bother me,
For I belong to somebody.
[Traditional song]

The Itsy Bitsy Spider
The itsy bitsy spider went up the water spout.
Down came the rain and washed the spider out.
Out came the sun and dried up all the rain.
So the itsy bitsy spider went up the spout again.
[Traditional]

Game

Ladybug Game
Children stand and face a partner.
Say this rhyme together, doing the actions.

Face to face.
Back to back.
Face to face.
Ladybug!

When they say ladybug they run around and choose a different partner. Repeat the rhyme.
[Virginia Brace]

Books to Share

Brandenberg, Franz. *Fresh Cider and Pie.* MacMillan, 1973. The spider catches a fly who outwits her with cider and pie.

Brown, Ruth. *Ladybug Ladybug.* Dutton, 1988. This adaptation of the nursery rhyme shows Ladybug meeting a variety of animals while rushing home to her children.

Carle, Eric. *Grouchy Ladybug.* Crowell, 1977. A grouchy ladybug who is looking for a fight challenges everyone she meets regardless of their size or strength.

Inkpen, Mick. *Billy's Beetle.* Harcourt Brace Jovanovich, 1992. Billy searches for his lost beetle,

assisted by both people and animals.

Pike, Norman. *The Peach Tree.* Stemmer House, 1983. When a peach tree is threatened by aphids, Farmer Parmeroy brings in some ladybugs to save the tree and retore the balance of nature.

Raffi. *Spider on the Floor.* Crown, 1993. The illustrated version of the Bill Russell song about the curious spider. Includes musical notation.

Trapani, Iza. *Itsy Bitsy Spider.* Whispering Coyote, 1993. The itsy bitsy spider encounters a fan, a mouse, a cat and a rocking chair as she makes her way to the top of a tree to spin her web.

Ladybug Magnet

End your storytime by helping the children make a ladybug magnet.

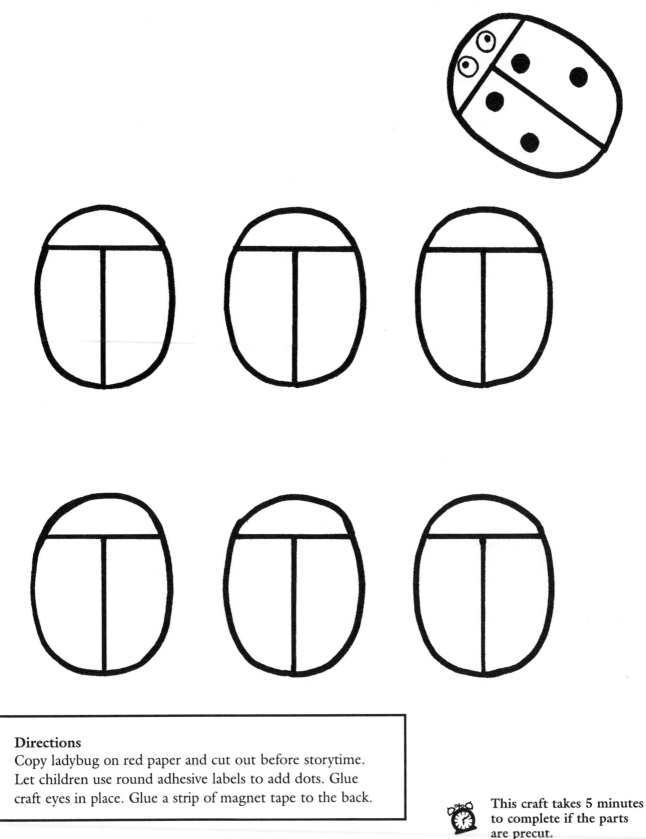

Directions
Copy ladybug on red paper and cut out before storytime. Let children use round adhesive labels to add dots. Glue craft eyes in place. Glue a strip of magnet tape to the back.

This craft takes 5 minutes to complete if the parts are precut.

Cats

Before Sharing Books

Use a kitten puppet or stuffed toy to introduce your theme. You may ask the children to name your kitten. As you pet the kitten in your lap, you may talk about what kittens like: They like to be held. They like to have their ears rubbed. They like to sleep in a warm, sunny window or on someone's bed. They do not like to have their tails pulled. They do not like to get wet. They do not like loud noises. Have the children get ready for stories by making a soft place on the rug to sit. Show children how kittens do this by using their paws.

Rest Activities

Fingerplays and Action Rhymes

Here Is a Kitty

Here is a Kitty with ears so pretty, *(hold up little and index fingers, place thumb over folded middle fingers)*

And here's her bowl of milk. *(curve other hand up like a bowl)*

She licks it up, *(make a licking motion with thumb over bowl)*

Then washes her fur. *(rub thumb over folded middle fingers)*

Settles down and starts to purr! *(turn bowl over, lay kitten on it)*

[Traditional]

Five Little Kittens

Five little kittens standing in a row. *(hold up five fingers)*

They nod their heads to the children, so. *(bend fingers slightly)*

They run to the left. *(move hand to the left)*

They run to the right. *(move hand to the right)*

They stand and stretch in the bright sunlight. *(open hand very wide)*

Along comes a dog, looking for some fun. *(bring other hand up, thumb touching fingers)*

Meowwww!

See those kittens run! *(put hands behind back)*

[Traditional]

Song

Pussy Cat, Pussy Cat

Pussy cat, pussy cat,
Where have you been?
I've been to London to visit the queen.
Pussy cat, pussy cat,
What did you there?
I frightened the little mouse under her chair.

[Traditional]

Books to Share

Astley, Judy. **When One Cat Woke Up.** Dial, 1990. A cat wakes up and romps through the house, wrecking things in numerical order.

Barton, Byron. **The Wee Little Woman.** HarperCollins, 1995. When a wee little woman milks her wee little cow and leaves a bowl of milk on her wee little table, the situation proves too tempting for a wee little cat.

Bernhard, Durga. **What's Maggie Up To?** Holiday House, 1992. The children in an apartment house wonder what the wandering cat, Maggie, is up to when she changes her behavior and disappears into the attic for days.

Casey, Patricia. **My Cat Jack.** Candlewick, 1994. A close-up look at the day-to-day doings of a pet cat.

Ehlert, Lois. **Feathers for Lunch.** Harcourt Brace Jovanovich, 1990. An escaped housecat encounters twelve birds in the backyard but fails to catch any of them and has to eat feathers for lunch.

Rose, Agatha. **Hide and Seek in the Yellow House.** Viking, 1992. A mischievous kitten leads his mother on a merry chase of hide-and-seek throughout their home.

Rylant, Cynthia. **Everyday Pets.** Bradbury, 1993. The bunnies, ducks, dogs, cats and other everyday pets enjoy sleeping in the sun, eating and making noise.

Paper Plate Cat

Finish your storytime by letting the children assemble a paper plate cat.

Directions
Using the pattern, cut an arch from a paper plate for the cat's body. Cut a tail from the center of the paper plate. Copy the head pattern and cut out. Let the children color the parts, then assemble them with glue.

 This craft takes **10 minutes to complete if the parts are precut.**

Chickens

Before Sharing Books

A barnyard scratch should get everyone in the mood for chicken stories. Read the poem, "Five Little Chickens." Then make chicken noises while you flap your elbows like chicken wings and scratch at the floor with your feet like chickens. Then settle everyone into a pretend nest so they can listen to the stories.

Rest Activities

Fingerplays and Action Rhymes

Hickety-Pickety

Hickety-Pickety my black hen.
She lays eggs for gentlemen.
Sometimes nine and sometimes ten.
Hickety-Pickety my black hen.

Hold up nine fingers, then ten fingers.
[Traditional]

Chicken Noises

Make a noise like a rooster.   *(Crow)*
Make a noise like a hen.   *(Cluck)*
Make a noise like a chick. *(Peep)*
Make a noise like an egg.   *(Silence)*

Five Little Chickens

Said the first little chicken,
With a queer little squirm,
"I wish I could find,
A fat little worm."

Said the next little chicken,
With an odd little shrug,
"I wish I could find,
A fat little slug."

Said the third little chicken,
With a sharp little squeal,
"I wish I could find,
Some nice yellow meal."

Said the fourth little chicken,
With a small sigh of grief,
"I wish I could find,
A little green leaf."

Said the fifth little chicken,
With a faint little moan,
"I wish I could find,
A wee gravel stone."

"Now see here, " said the mother,
From the green garden patch,
"If you want your breakfast,
Just come here and scratch."
[Traditional]

Books to Share

Baker, Keith. *Big Fat Hen.* Harcourt Brace 1994. Big Fat Hen counts to ten with her friends and their chicks.

Edwards, Michelle. *Chicken Man.* Lothrop Lee & Shepard, 1991. Each time Chicken Man is moved into a new job on the kibbutz, someone else wants to take it instead, and the chickens suffer the consequences.

Ginsburg, Mirra. *Good Morning, Chick.* Greenwillow, 1980. When he tries to imitate a rooster, a newly-hatched chick falls in a puddle.

Hobson, Sally. *Chicken Little.* Simon and Schuster, 1994. Chicken Little tells her friends the sky is falling.

Reiser, Lynn. *The Surprise Family.* Greenwillow, 1994. A baby chicken accepts a young boy as her mother, and later becomes a surrogate mother for some ducklings she has hatched.

Kasza, Keiko. *The Wolf's Chicken Stew.* Putnam, 1987. A wolf who likes to cook wants to make chicken stew but ends up making food for the chicks.

Stoeke, Janet Morgan. *A Hat for Minerva Louise.* Dutton, 1994. Minerva Louise, a snow-loving chicken, mistakes a pair of mittens for two hats to keep both ends warm.

Fuzzy Chick

Help the children make a chick from an egg shell.

Directions

Crack eggs and save the egg shells. You will need a half shell for each child. Copy and cut out feet from yellow paper. Glue the feet to the bottom of each egg shell before story-time. You may draw the chicken face on the egg ahead of time with marker, or allow the children to do it in story-time. Let the children glue a cotton ball inside the egg shell. Pour a little water on the cotton ball. Sprinkle it with grass seed. Tell the children to keep it moist and in a few days the chicken will grow green fuzz.

If you have one prepared ahead that is already growing grass it will let them know what theirs will look like soon.

 This craft takes 5 minutes to complete.

China

Before Sharing Books

Teach the children to bow, as this is the way people show respect for each other in China. Show them a bowl of uncooked rice. Let them feel it. Tell them this is an important food in China, and that a person who has plenty of rice feels rich. When everyone is seated, exchange bows once more and begin your stories.

Rest Activities

Fingerplays and Action Rhymes

Five Little Pandas

Five little pandas went out to play,

On a sunny, sunny day. *(hold up five fingers)*

The first little panda climbed a tree. *(hand over hand)*

The second little panda got stung by a bee. *(poke finger on stomach—pull away. Ouch!)*

The third little panda went rolling down hill. *(rolling motion with hands)*

The fourth little panda sat oh, so still. *(hold index finger to lips — Shh!)*

The fifth little panda went to the river,

And got so wet he had to shiver! *(hug and shiver)*

Songs

We Like Rice *Tune of: "Three Blind Mice"*

We like rice. We like rice. *(rub tummy)*

Rice is nice. Rice is nice. *(point to smiling face)*

We eat some rice almost every day. *(pretend to eat with chopsticks)*

It gives us energy so we can play. *(run in place)*

And when we are full we like to say, *(rub tummy)*

"We like rice."

[Adapted traditional song]

Chinese Lantern *Tune of: "I'm A Little Tea Pot"*

I'm a Chinese lantern shining bright. *(open and close one hand a few times)*

Use me to light your way at night. *(hand above eyes and look around)*

If it's really dark, just light one more. *(open and close two hands a few times)*

That's what Chinese lanterns are for. *(point with index finger)*

[Adapted traditional song]

Books to Share

Demi. *The Stonecutter.* Crown, 1995. A stonecutter wants to be everything he is not and learns the hard way that what he really wants to be is exactly who he is.

Flack, Marjorie. *The Story About Ping.* Puffin, 1961. A duck is too late to get back to his master's house boat on the Yangtze river.

Hong, Lily Toy. *How the Ox Star Fell From Heaven.* Whitman, 1991. This Chinese folktale explains why the ox became a beast of burden.

———. *Two of Everything.* Whitman, 1993. A poor Chinese farmer finds a brass pot that duplicates everything that is placed inside it.

Rappaport, Doreen. *The Long-Haired Girl: A Chinese Legend.* Dial, 1995. Ah-mei challenges the God of Thunder who then gives her parched village will have water for planting crops.

Torre, Betty L. *The Luminous Pearl: A Chinese Folktale.* Orchard, 1990. Two brothers go on a quest for a luminous pearl in order to win the Dragon King's beautiful daughter for a wife.

Yep, Laurence. *The Boy Who Swallowed Snakes.* Scholastic, 1994. A boy tries to get rid of the snakes that have come with the bowl of silver coins he found.

Yolen, Jane. *The Emperor and the Kite.* Philomel, 1988. When the emperor is imprisoned in a high tower, his smallest daughter uses her kite to save him.

———. *Little Plum.* Philomel, 1994. An old Chinese couple has a son who never grows any larger than a plum seed, but his size does not prevent him from saving his village.

———. *Lon Po Po: A Red-Riding Hood Story from China.* Philomel, 1989. Three sisters staying home alone are endangered by a hungry wolf who is disguised as their grandmother.

Chinese Lantern

After your stories, help the children make a paper lantern. This craft requires five minutes if parts are precut. Older children may be able to cut the lantern parts themselves.

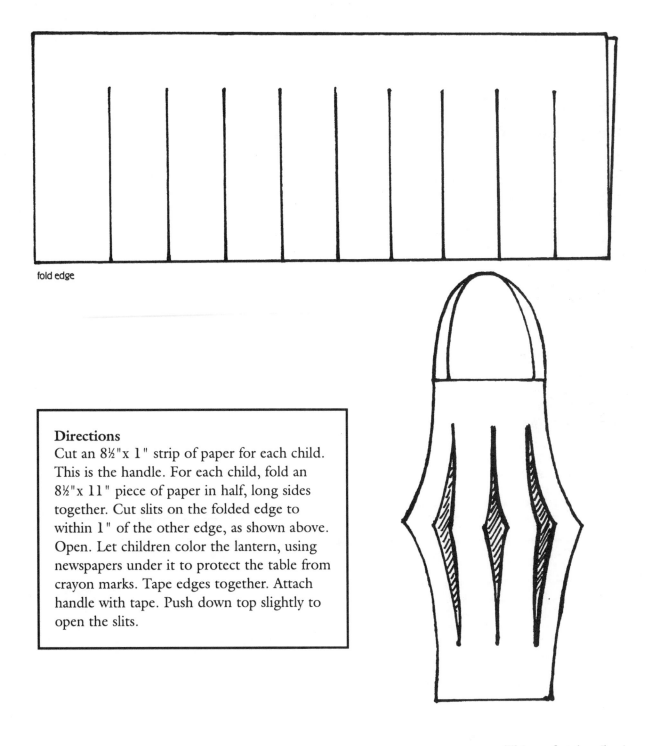

fold edge

Directions

Cut an 8½"x 1" strip of paper for each child. This is the handle. For each child, fold an 8½"x 11" piece of paper in half, long sides together. Cut slits on the folded edge to within 1" of the other edge, as shown above. Open. Let children color the lantern, using newspapers under it to protect the table from crayon marks. Tape edges together. Attach handle with tape. Push down top slightly to open the slits.

 This craft takes 5 minutes to complete if the parts are precut.

COWS

Before Sharing Books

Lead the children in a series of barnyard activities, such as feeding the chickens, opening the gate, jumping over a mud puddle, and milking a cow. Settle everyone down in the barn for some cow stories. Hoedown music adds a nice touch to this storytime opening.

Rest Activities

Fingerplays and Action Rhymes

Slow, Slow Cow

Slow, slow cow, *(walk slowly in place)*
Don't you know how, *(shake head)*
To hurry to the barn,
Where it's nice and warm? *(run quickly in place)*
[Traditional]

Little Boy Blue

Little boy blue, come blow your horn. *(put fist to lips)*
The sheep's in the meadow, *(draw curly wool around head with fingers)*
The cow's in the corn. *(put index fingers to head like horns)*
Where is the boy who looks after the sheep? *(put hand to forehead and search)*
He's under the haystack, fast asleep. *(lay head on hands and snore)*
[Traditional rhyme, actions added]

Song

The Bell On the Cow

Tune of: "The Wheels on the Bus"
The bell on the cow goes,
Clang, clang, clang.
Clang, clang, clang.
Clang, clang, clang.
The bell on the cow goes,
Clang, clang, clang,
All the way home.

Additional Verses

The tail on the cow goes,
Swish, swish, swish.

The eyes on the cow go,
Blink, blink, blink.
[Adapted traditional song]

Books to Share

Dubanovich, Arlene. *Calico Cows.* Viking, 1993. The misadventures of a group of cows who must learn to think for themselves when their leader is taken to the county fair.

Eagle, Kin. *Hey, Diddle Diddle.* Whispering Coyote, 1997. This nonsense tale continues the story of the traditional rhyme in which the cow jumps over the moon.

Harrison, David. *When the Cows Come Home.* Boyds Mills, 1994. A herd of cows rides bicycles, square dances, goes swimming, and more in this story in rhyme.

Johnson, Paul Brett. *The Cow Who Wouldn't Come Down.* Orchard, 1993. Miss Rosemary tries everything to coax her flying cow Gertrude down from the sky.

Lesser, Carolyn. *What a Wonderful Day to Be a Cow.* Knopf, 1995. Every month of the year, the animals on the farm enjoy their way of life and the weather that greets them.

Lindbergh, Reeve. *There's a Cow in the Road!* Dial, 1993. A girl preparing for school is surprised by the number of farm animals gathering in the road outside.

Most, Bernard. *The Cow That Went Oink.* Harcourt, Brace, 1990. A cow that oinks and a pig that moos are teased by the other animals until each teaches the other a new sound. Also: *Cock-a-Doodle-Moo!*

Cow Necklace

Complete your visit to the barnyard by helping the children decorate a cow necklace. This craft takes five minutes to complete. You may want to ask for parent volunteers to help with the stamp pads and cleaning up their thumbs.

Directions

Copy cow shape on stiff paper and cut out. Punch a hole with a single hole punch in the back where marked. Cut a 24" piece of yarn or string for each child. Let the children put spots on their cow with thumb prints. Use a water-based stamp pad, if available, for easier clean up. Wipe off the child's thumb. Let the children put a string through the hole of the cow. Tie the ends together to make a necklace.

 This craft takes 5 minutes to complete.

Dinosaurs

Before Sharing Books

Hang vines on the door to your storytime room. These can be artificial garlands or just strips of green crepe paper. As you walk through the vines, tell the children they are walking back in time to the days of the dinosaurs.

Rest Activities

Fingerplays and Action Rhymes

Five Baby Dinosaurs

One baby dinosaur began to roar,
"I want to eat some more, some more!" *(hold up one finger for each dinosaur)*

Two baby dinosaurs began to roar,
"We want to eat some more, some more!"

Three baby dinosaurs began to roar,
"We want to eat some more, some more!"

Four baby dinosaurs began to roar,
"We want to eat some more, some more!"

Five baby dinosaurs began to roar,
Five baby dinosaurs ate so much more, *(wiggle all the fingers)*

That they all fell asleep and began to snore. *(bend fingers down and loudly snore)*

[Adapted traditional]

A Dinosaur Came Into Town

A dinosaur came into town. **Oh my!** *(children say "Oh my" and put both hands up to cheeks each time)*

He stomped and stomped and stomped around. **Oh my!**

He ate a bush. He ate a tree. **Oh my!**

And started looking right at me. **Oh my!**

He lifted his head to the sky so blue. **Oh my!**

And then he sneezed! *Ah Ah Ah Choo!* **Oh my!**

He blew me far, far away. **Oh my!**

But I like it here, so I think I'll stay. **Oh my!**

Song

Baby Dinosaur
Tune of: "Arkansas Traveler"
Oh, I'm bringing home a baby dinosaur.
Won't my mother go right through the floor!
Oh, I'm bringing home a baby dinosaur.
Ouch. He stepped on my toe and made it sore.
[Adapted traditional song]

Books to Share

Barton, Byron. ***Bones, Bones, Dinosaur Bones.*** Crowell, 1990. A cast of characters looks for, finds and assembles some dinosaur bones.

Birney, Betty. ***Tyrannosaurus Tex.*** Houghton Mifflin, 1994. Tyrannosaurus Tex, a dinosaur cowboy, helps Cookie and Pete put out a prairie fire and scare away some cattle rustlers.

Boynton, Sandra. ***Oh My, Oh My, Dinosaurs!*** Workman, 1993. Die-cut pages show dinosaurs sunbathing and creating art in this story in rhyme.

Hartmann, Wendy. ***The Dinosaurs Are Back, and It's All Your Fault, Edward!*** McElderry, 1997. Edward gets nervous as his older brother tries to convince him that a dinosaur egg is about to hatch under his bed.

Sierra, Judy. ***Good Night, Dinosaurs.*** Clarion, 1996. Verses describe the bedtime preparations of different kinds of dinosaurs.

Stickland, Paul. ***Dinosaur Roar!*** Dutton, 1994. Rhyming text presents all kinds of dinosaurs, including ones that are sweet, grumpy, spiky and lumpy.

Threadgall, Collin. ***Dinosaur Fright.*** Tambourine, 1993. When bullying brachiosaurs invade the home of smaller dinosaurs, a little nanosaur develops a clever plan.

Wilson, Sarah. ***Good Zap, Little Grog.*** Candlewick, 1995. A fanciful view of a day in the life of little Grog.

Dinosaur Sandwiches

Invite adults to have a dinosaur lunch with their child, and help put together the dinosaur sandwiches.

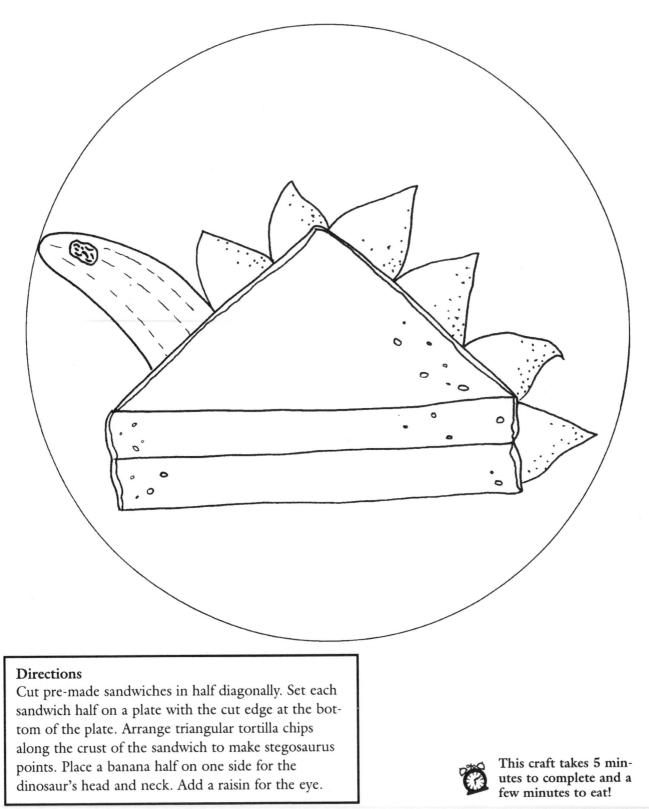

Directions

Cut pre-made sandwiches in half diagonally. Set each sandwich half on a plate with the cut edge at the bottom of the plate. Arrange triangular tortilla chips along the crust of the sandwich to make stegosaurus points. Place a banana half on one side for the dinosaur's head and neck. Add a raisin for the eye.

This craft takes 5 minutes to complete and a few minutes to eat!

Dogs

Before Sharing Books

Use a dog puppet to introduce your theme. Have the puppet tell about an adventure he had chasing a cat, about the time when he was just a puppy and he chewed up his little boy's shoe, and about his favorite way to cool off in the summer by digging a cool hole in the dirt. Then the puppet can ask the children if they would like to hear some stories about some of his friends.

Rest Activities

Fingerplays and Action Rhymes

Hey Diddle Diddle

Hey diddle diddle,
The cat and the fiddle,
The cow jumped over the moon.
The little dog laughed to see such a sport,
And the dish ran away with the spoon.
[Traditional]

Songs

Do Your Ears Hang Low?

Do your ears hang low?
Do they wabble to and fro?
Can you tie them in a knot?
Can you tie them in a bow?
Can you throw them over your shoulder,
Like a continental soldier?
Do your ears hang low?
[Traditional song]

Longer version in: **The World's Best Funny Songs** *by Esther Nelson. Sterling, 1988.*

How Much Is That Doggie?

How much is that doggie in the window?
The one with the waggely tail?
How much is that doggie in the window?
I do hope that doggie's for sale.
[Traditional song]

This Old Man

This old man, he played one.
He played knick knack on my thumb.
With a knick knack paddy whack,
Give a dog a bone.
This old man came rolling home.
[Traditional song]

Oh Where, Oh Where Has My Little Dog Gone?

Oh where, oh where has my little dog gone?
Oh where, oh where can he be?
With his tail cut short and his ears cut long?
Oh where, oh where can he be?
[Traditional song]

Longer version in: **Jane Yolen's Old MacDonald Songbook.** *Boyds Mills, 1988.*

Books to Share

Asch, Frank. *The Last Puppy.* Little Simon, 1980. The last born of nine puppies worries that he will be the last chosen as a pet.

Hill, Eric. *Spot Sleeps Over.* Putnam, 1990. Spot sleeps over at Steve's house. He forgets to take something very important, but luckily his mom saves the day. Also: *Spot Goes to the Park* and *Where's Spot?*

Inkpen, Mick. *Kipper.* Little, Brown, 1992. Tired of his old blanket and basket, Kipper the dog searches among the animals outside for a place to sleep. Also: *Kipper's Toybox* and *Kipper's Birthday*

Gackenbach, Dick. *Claude Has a Picnic.* Clarion,

1993. After resolving his neighbor's problems, Claude the dog joins them in a picnic. Also: *What's Claude Doing?* and *Claude and Pepper*

Gliori, Debi. *The Snow Lambs.* Scholastic, 1996. Because she is on a rescue mission, Bess, the sheep dog, fails to respond when called home as a winter storm approaches.

Hazelaar, Cor. *Dogs Everywhere.* Knopf, 1995. Dogs of all sorts are walked in the park.

Janovitz, Marilyn. *Bowl Patrol!* North-South, 1996. Rhyming words tell how a vigilant sheepdog tries to protect his water dish.

Dog House

Finish up your dog storytime by helping the children give their dog a home in a doghouse.

Directions
Copy the doghouse on colored paper and cut out. Copy the dog in the doghouse door on white paper and cut out before storytime. Let the children paste the doghouse door on the doghouse. Let them color the dog.

 This craft takes 10 minutes to complete.

Elephants

Before Sharing Books

Tell the children you are thinking of an animal that has a tail like a rope, ears like fans, feet like frying pans and a nose like a hose. You may want to bring a rope, fan, pan and garden hose to show them. When they have guessed that your animal is elephant, parade them around the room in an elephant walk, then sit them down for stories.

Rest Activities

Fingerplays and Action Rhymes

The Elephant

An elephant goes like this and that. *(stamp feet)*
He's terribly big, *(raise arms)*
And he's terribly fat. *(spread arms wide)*
He has no fingers, *(wiggle fingers)*
He has no toes, *(touch toes)*
But goodness, gracious, what a nose! *(draw hands out like a long curly trunk)*
[Traditional]

Poem

"Holding Hands" from *Read Aloud Rhymes for the Very Young* by Jack Prelutsky. (Knopf, 1986)

Song

Baby Elephants
Tune of: "Mary Had a Little Lamb
Baby elephants like to walk,
In a line, tail to trunk.
Trunk to tail and tail to trunk.
That's how baby elephants walk.

Reach back, between legs with one hand, and reach forward with the other hand. Hold on to the hand in front of you and the one behind you, forming a chain of baby elephants. Walk around the room.

Books to Share

Appelt, Kathi. *Elephants Aloft.* Harcourt Brace Jovanovich, 1993. Two elephants travel to Africa to visit their Aunt Rwanda.

Deetlefs, Rene. *Tabu and the Dancing Elephants.* Dutton, 1995, When a young boy named Tabu is taken away by an old mama elephant while his father is sleeping, Tabu's mother gets him back by teaching the elephants to dance.

Ford, Miela. *Little Elephant.* Greenwillow, 1994. Captioned photographs depict a young elephant's adventures playing in the water.

Riddell, Chris. *The Trouble with Elephants.* Harper Trophy, 1990. A little girl describes the various problems with elephants, but decides that the real trouble is that you can't help but love them.

Sheppard, Jeff. *The Right Number of Elephants.* Harper & Row, 1990. A counting book in which a little girl relies on the help of some eager elephants.

West, Colin. *One Little Elephant.* Candlewick, 1994. As an elephant is joined by others, one at a time, the reader may count from one to ten.

Peanut Pick-Up

Finish your elephant storytime by helping the children make an elephant that can pick up a peanut. This craft takes five minutes to complete, if all parts are precut. Allow time to play Peanut Pick-Up.

cut lines

Directions

Copy and cut out peanut and elephant for each child. Cut slits at trunk and hat on dark line before storytime. Let the children color the elephant and bend the ears forward. Insert a straw into the slits. The elephant will pick up the peanut when the child sucks the straw.

This craft takes 5 minutes to complete if all the parts are precut.

Fathers

Before Sharing Books

Invite one or more fathers to storytime. Ask them to be prepared to tell about a favorite memory from their childhood. Ask them questions such as, "When you were five years old, what did you want to be when you grew up?" "What do you like best about being a dad?" or "What is your favorite fun activity that you do with your child?"

Rest Activities

Fingerplays and Action Rhymes

My Dad

Tall as a tree out in my yard. *(reach up high)*
Strong as can be, he works so hard. *(flex muscles)*
He can lift me up so high. *(bend down low, lift arms above head)*
He's my Dad. He's quite a guy. *(point to self)*

Songs

Dad and I Do Lots of Work
Tune of: "Row, Row, Row Your Boat"
Paint, paint, paint the fence,
See what we can do.
Dad and I do lots of work. It is fun to do.

Wash, wash, wash the car,
See what we can do.
Dad and I do lots of work. It is fun to do.

Rake, rake, rake the leaves,
See what we can do.
Dad and I do lots of work. It is fun to do.
[Adapted traditional song]

Hush, Little Baby

Hush little baby, don't say a word,
Daddy's going to buy you a mocking bird.

And if that mocking bird won't sing,
Daddy's going to buy you a golden ring.

And if that golden ring turns brass,
Daddy's going to buy you a looking glass.

And if that looking glass gets broke,
Daddy's going to buy you a billy-goat.

And if that billy-goat won't pull,
Daddy's going to buy you a cart and bull.

And if that cart and bull turns over,
Daddy's going to buy you a dog named Rover.

And if that dog named Rover won't bark,
Daddy's going to buy you a horse and cart.

And if that horse and cart fall down,
You'll still be the sweetest child in town.
[Traditional]

Books to Share

Butterworth, Nick. *My Dad Is Brilliant.* Discovery Books, 1989. Dad is strong as a gorilla, a marvelous cook, and he can sing like a pop star.

Gardella, Tricia. *Just Like My Dad.* HarperCollins, 1993. A young child glories in the sights, sounds, smells, and activities of a day spent working on a cattle ranch as a cowhand, just like Dad.

Lakin, Pat. *Dad and Me in the Morning.* Whitman, 1994. A deaf boy and his father share a special time as they watch the sun rise at the beach.

Jennings, Dana Andrew. *Me, Dad and Number 6.* Harcourt Brace, 1997. A father, his friends, and his six-year-old son rebuild an old car and drive it in races.

London, Jonathan. *Old Salt, Young Salt.* Lothrop, Lee & Shepard, 1996. Aaron's Dad is an experienced sailor, and Aaron must find his sea legs when they go out together for a day of fishing on the bay.

Parker, Kristy. *My Dad the Magnificent.* Dutton, 1987. Although Buddy exaggerates a bit about his magnificent father, the good times they share on a Saturday morning show that his father really is great.

Pringle, Laurence. *Octopus Hug.* Boyds Mills, 1993. When Mom goes out for the evening, Dad and the kids invent games filled with fun and laughter, and they all learn how to give an octopus hug.

Wyeth, Sharon Dennis. *Always My Dad.* Knopf, 1995. Although she doesn't get to see her father very often, a girl enjoys the time she and her brothers spend with him one summer while visiting their grandparents' farm.

Pom-Pom Game

After your stories, help the children make a game to play with their fathers.

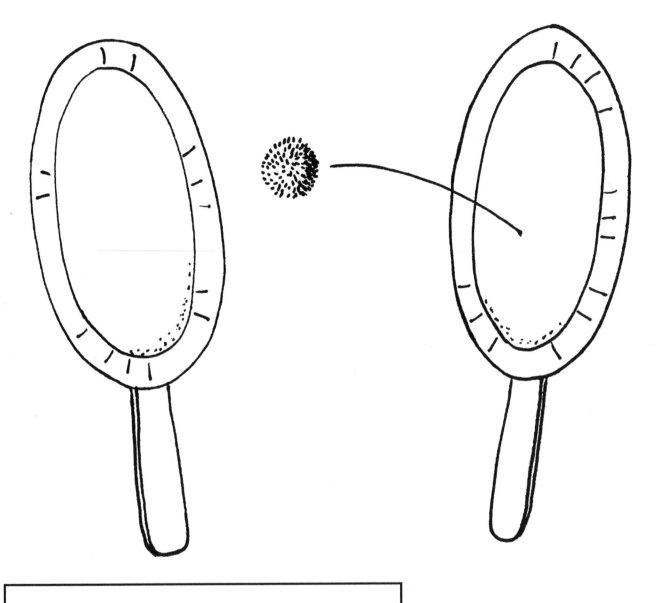

Directions
Tape paint stirring sticks to the back of strong paper plates using strapping tape or other strong tape. You will need two per child. Let the children decorate the paper plates with markers. To play the game, child and father hit a pom pom back and forth, using the paper plates as rackets.

 This craft takes 10 minutes to complete.

Fish

Before Sharing Books

Play a guessing game with the children. Say, "I am thinking of an animal that is a good swimmer, comes in many beautiful colors, lives in the water, and has fins and scales." Ask the children to raise their hands when they know what you are thinking of. You may wish to bring a bowl of goldfish as a visual aid for this storytime. Bring it out after they have guessed.

Rest Activities

Fingerplays and Action Rhymes

I hold my fingers like a fish, *(place palms of hands together)*
And wave them as I go. *(wiggle hands)*
See them swimming with a swish, *(move quickly forward)*
So swiftly to and fro. *(move to the left, then to the right)*
[Traditional]

Songs

I Wish I Was a Fishy
Tune of: "If You're Happy and You Know It"
Oh, I wish I was a fishy in the sea.
Oh, I wish I was a fishy in the sea.
I'd swim around so cute,
without my bathing suit.
Oh, I wish I was a fishy in the sea.
[Traditional song]

I'm a Little Fishy
Tune of: "I'm a little Teapot"
I'm a little fishy,
I can swim.
Here is my tail and here is my fin.

When I want to have some fun
with my friends,
I wiggle my tail and jump right in.
[Adapted traditional song]

Books to Share

Clements, Andrew. *Big Al*. Picture Book Studio, 1988. Big Al tries to hide his scary appearance, because even though he is gentle and friendly the smaller fish are afraid of him until he proves that he is a true friend.

Ehlert, Lois. *Fish Eyes*. Harcourt Brace Jovanovich, 1990. This colorful counting book depicts the fish a child might see if he turned into a fish himself.

Kalan, Robert. *Blue Sea*. Greenwillow, 1979. Fish of varying sizes introduce space and size relationships.

MacDonald, Suse. *Sea Shapes*. Harcourt Brace, 1994. Crescent, star, spiral and other shapes can be found in sea creatures such as sperm whales, butterfly fish and jellyfish.

Pfister, Marcus. *Rainbow Fish*. North-South Books, 1995. The most beautiful fish in the ocean discovers the real value of personal beauty and friendship. Also: *Rainbow Fish to the Rescue*

Fish Bowl

Make a fish bowl at the end of your storytime. There are two options for this craft to suit the age of your storytime group. Prepare the fish bowls before storytime. The color and cut activity will take ten minutes. The trace and color activity will take five.

Directions

Cut bowl of blue construction paper using pattern before storytime. Let the child color fish, cut out, and glue fish on the bowl. Add reinforcement rings for bubbles and confetti for gravel.

Alternate craft for ages 2–3: Copy fish bowl on blue paper and cut out before storytime. Trace child's hand in the center of the fish bowl. The thumb is the fin, the fingers are the tail. Draw on an eye and a mouth. Let the child color the fish.

This craft takes 5–10 minutes to complete.

France

Before Sharing Books

Bring a chef's hat, or make one of paper. Ask a child to wear the hat and be the chef for the day. Tell the children that the group is going to make soup. Let them suggest, one at a time, something good to put into the soup. They may pantomime adding it to the pot, while the chef stirs it up. Say, "I know a story from France about making soup. All of today's stories come from France." You may wish to show them where it is on a map.

Rest Activities

Fingerplays and Action Rhymes

Merci

I can say thanks.
Merci. Merci. [mār-SĒ]
Thanks to you. *(shake hands with person on left)*
To you, Merci. *(shake hands with person on right)*

Hello

Bonjour, bonjour. [bōn-ZHUR] *(wave left hand)*
Hello, hello. *(wave right hand)*
People are friendly, *(smile)*
Wherever you go. *(sweep arm left to right)*

Rainbow

I know a rainbow,
A rainbow of colors!
Rouge, orange, jaune, vert, bleu!
[roozh, or-AHZH, zhōn, vār, bleuh]
Red, orange, yellow, green, blue! *(point to colors around the room as you say them)*

Song

Stir the Soup

Tune of: "Row, Row, Row Your boat"

Stir, stir, stir the soup, *(stirring motion)*
Taste a little sip. *(pretend to sip from a spoon)*
A pinch of this, a bunch of that, *(pretend to add to the pot)*
To give a little zip. *(snap fingers on the word zip)*
[Adapted traditional song]

Books to Share

Fischer, Hans *Puss in Boots: A Fairy Tale*. North-South, 1996. A clever cat helps his poor master win fame, fortune, and the hand of a beautiful princess.

Hansard, Peter. *Jig, Fig and Mrs. Pig*. Candlewick, 1995. A young pig is punished for his rudeness and his hard-working female servant is rewarded.

Huck, Charlotte S. *Toads and Diamonds*. Greenwillow, 1996. Two step-sisters receive appropriate gifts for their actions: one's words are accompanied by flowers and jewels, the other's by toads and snakes.

Kimmel, Eric. *Three Sacks of Truth: A Story from France*. Holiday House, 1993. With the aid of a perfect peach, a silver fife, and his own resources, Petit Jean outwits a dishonest king and wins the hand of a princess.

Mayer, Marianna. *Beauty and the Beast*. Four Winds, 1978. Through her great ability to love, a kind girl releases a handsome prince from the spell which has made him an ugly beast.

Meyers, Odette. *The Enchanted Umbrella*. Harcourt Brace Jovanovich, 1988. Patou escapes from danger and finds fame and fortune with the aid of a magic umbrella.

Patron, Susan. *Burgoo Stew*. Orchard, 1991. A variation of "Stone Soup" in which old Billy Que tames a group of rough, hungry boys.

VanRynbach, Iris. *The Soup Stone*. Greenwillow, 1988. When a family claims it has no food to feed him, a hungry soldier helps them make soup from a stone and water.

Enchanted Umbrella

Help the children make an enchanted umbrella to take home.

Directions

Using the pattern, cut an umbrella shape in the middle of an 8½"x 11" sheet of black construction paper for each child. Give the children a sheet of white paper to color. Let them do a free design or scribble design on the white paper. Glue the black umbrella-shaped frame over the colored design so the colors show through. Glue a candy cane below the umbrella for a handle.

This craft takes 5 minutes to complete if the umbrella is precut.

Frogs

Before Sharing Books

Use a frog puppet or picture to introduce your storytime theme. Ask the children if they know where frogs live, what they like to eat, and what noise they make. Lead them in a short hop around the storytime room, then settle everyone down with each child on a his own imaginary lilly pad to hear some stories about frogs.

Rest Activities

Fingerplays and Action Rhymes

Five Little Frogs

Five little frogs sitting on a log. *(hold up five fingers)*

This little frog is still a polywog. *(point to thumb)*

This little frog wears a happy grin. *(point to index finger)*

This little frog is tall and thin. *(point to tall finger)*

This little frog can jump real high. *(point to ring finger)*

This little frog wants to fly. *(point to little finger)*

So he calls out "Ribbit!" and a bird flies by,

And takes him for a ride way up to the sky! *(make wings with both hands)*

Froggies Splash

Five little froggies sitting by a pool. *(cup hands)*

One went splash! In the water so cool. *(raise one finger then jump once)*

Froggies splash high, *(raise hands and wave above head while jumping)*

Froggies splash low, *(lower hand to the floor while jumping)*

Froggies splash everywhere, to and fro. *(wave arms and jump in all directions)*

Hoppity Hop

A little green frog in a pond am I. *(point to self)*

Hoppity, hoppity hop. *(hop three times)*

I sit on a leaf, high and dry, *(squat down)*

And watch all the fishes as they swim by. *(put hands together and move them like a fish)*

Splash! How I make the water fly! *(arms circle up as you stand up)*

Hoppity, hoppity, hop. *(hop three times)*
[Traditional]

Books to Share

Arnold, Tedd. ***Green Wilma.*** Dial, 1993. Waking up with a frog-like appearance, Wilma is disruptive at school as she searches for some tasty flies.

Gordon, Margaret. ***Frogs' Holiday.*** Viking Kestrel, 1986. Some frogs leave their noisy pond to search for a perfect place for a holiday and find a warm, damp launderette to be just perfect.

Kalan, Robert. ***Jump, Frog, Jump.*** Greenwillow, 1981. A frog gets away from a fish, a snake and a turtle by jumping.

Maris, Ron. ***Better Move On, Frog.*** Franklin Watts, 1982. A frog finds badgers, rabbits, owls, mice and bees already occupying the holes he finds until he comes to a perfect hole for himself.

Shannon, George. ***April Showers.*** Greenwillow, 1995. A group of frogs enjoy dancing in the rain so much that they seem not to notice a snake sneaking up on them.

Walsh, Ellen Stoll. ***Hop, Jump.*** Harcourt Brace Jovanovich, 1993. Bored with just hopping and jumping, a frog discovers dancing.

Jumping Frogs

Make a jumping frog at the end of your storytime.

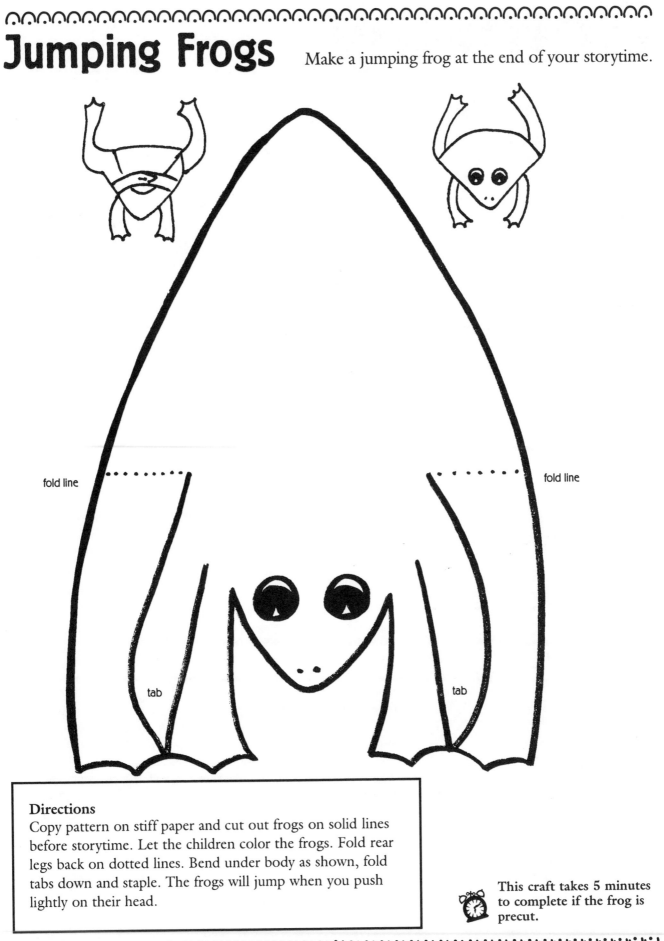

fold line

fold line

tab

tab

Directions

Copy pattern on stiff paper and cut out frogs on solid lines before storytime. Let the children color the frogs. Fold rear legs back on dotted lines. Bend under body as shown, fold tabs down and staple. The frogs will jump when you push lightly on their head.

This craft takes 5 minutes to complete if the frog is precut.

Germany

Before Sharing Books

Introduce this storytime with creative dramatics. Say, "Can you guess what story this is? Let's be tall trees in a forest." Have most of the children raise their arms high like tree branches. Select a girl and a boy. Walk them through the forrest, and let them drop bread crumbs, which will show them the way home. It is dark, and they go to sleep in the forrest. Use a bird puppet to eat up the bread crumbs while they are sleeping. Now they wake up and find out their bread crumbs are gone. Ask, "Who can guess what story this is?" Tell them Hansel and Gretel, and all of your stories today, come from Germany.

Rest Activities

Fingerplays and Action Rhymes

Counting in German
Ein, zwei, drei! [īn, tsvī, drī]
One, two, three.
I can count in German.
Count with me!

German Fruit
What do you like to eat?
Bananen, bananen! [bah-NĂ-něn] *(pretend to peel a banana)*
What do you like to eat?
Apfel. Apfel. [ĂP-fěl] *(rub apple on your shirt, then bite it)*
Yum!

Rapunzel
Rapunzel was a lovely girl. *(place hands by face)*
She lived in a tall, tall tower. *(reach high)*
A handsome prince came riding by, *(pretend to ride a horse)*
To visit for an hour. *(talking motion with both hands)*
He called up to her window, *(hand by mouth, look up)*
"Please let down your hair."
Out of the window came her long, long braid. *(pretend to brush hair from head down to feet)*
He climbed up, up to his lady fair. *(pretend to climb hand over hand)*

Books to Share

Bailey, Philip H. *The Wedding of Mistress Fox.* North-South, 1994. As she rejects suitor after suitor, the recently widowed Mistress Fox almost gives up on finding a new husband with the same wonderful qualities as the late Mr. Fox.

Berenzy, Alix. *Rapunzel.* Holt, 1995. A beautiful girl with long, golden hair is kept imprisoned in a lonely tower by a witch.

Byrd, Robert. *The Bear and the Bird King.* Dutton, 1994. When the bear insults the children of the Bird King, a war develops between the creatures of the ground and the creatures of the air.

Geringer, Laura. *The Seven Ravens.* HarperCollins, 1994. A little girl walks to the end of the world to find her seven brothers and free them from enchantment.

Grim, Jacob. *The Wolf and the Seven Little Kids.*

North-South, 1995. When six of her seven kids are swallowed by a wicked wolf, Old Mother Goat devises a way to rescue them.

Kimmel, Eric. *Iron John.* Holiday House, 1994. With the help of Iron John, the wild man of the forest who is under a curse, a young prince makes his way in the world and finds his true love.

Marshall, James. *Hansel and Gretel.* Penguin, 1994. A retelling of the folktale about two children who try to escape from the home of a wicked witch deep in the forest.

Ray, Jane. *The Twelve Dancing Princesses.* Dutton, 1996. A retelling of a traditional tale of how the king's twelve daughters wear out their shoes every night while supposedly sleeping in their locked bedroom.

Hansel & Gretel

Finish up your storytime with a maze and coloring sheet. Help Hansel and Gretel find their way back home.

Can you help Hansel and Gretel find their way home?

🕐 This craft takes 5 minutes to complete.

Halloween

Before Sharing Books

Invite children to come in costume for this storytime. Play a sound-effects tape or organ music as the children come in. Hang cobwebs and spiders in the room. Invite the children into your pretend haunted house for storytime. Ask them to tell you what kinds of spooky things they would expect to see in the haunted house. Ask them to watch for a ghost, a skeleton and a monster in the books that will be read today.

Rest Activities

Fingerplays and Action Rhymes

Who Said Boo?: Halloween Poems for the Very Young by Nancy White Carlstrom (Simon & Schuster, 1995). Monsters, witches, haunted houses and jack-o'-lanterns are the subject of these poems.

Two Little Ghosts

A very old witch was stirring a pot. *(make a stirring motion)*
Ooo-ooo! Ooo-ooo!

Two little ghosts said,
"What has she got?" *(put hands on hips, bend over as if looking into pot)*
Ooo-ooo! Ooo-ooo!

Tiptoe. Tiptoe. Tiptoe. *(make fingers creep forward in the air)*
Boo! *(raise hands high over head and jump)*
[Traditional]

Right Here in My Pocket

Right here in my pocket is a big surprise for you. *(point to shirt)*
It's not a wiggly spider, *(make fingers wiggle)*
Or a monster who says "Boo!" *(raise hands and say boo)*
It's not an umbrella, *(palm of one hand covers index finger of the other)*
Or a snake who likes to hiss. *(make hand and arm wiggle like a snake)*
Right here in my pocket, *(point to shirt)*
Is a big two-handed kiss. *MMMMwah!* *(blow a kiss)*
[Traditional]

Books to Share

Brown, Ruth. *A Dark, Dark Tale.* Dial, 1981. Journeying through a dark, dark house, a black cat surprises the only inhabitant at this abandoned house.

Galdone, Paul. *King of the Cats: A Ghost Story.* Seabury, 1980. As the gravedigger tells his wife how a band of cats marched into the cemetery to mourn their dead king, their own cat, Old Tom, listens attentively.

Glassman, Peter. *My Working Mom.* Morrow Junior, 1994. A young girl decides it is all right for her mother to work as a witch.

Hall, Zoe. *It's Pumpkin Time.* Scholastic, 1994. A sister and brother plant and tend their own pumpkin patch so they will have jack-o'-lanterns for Halloween.

Stutson, Caroline. *By the Light of the Halloween Moon.* Lothrop Lee & Shepard, 1993. A cumulative story with a host of Halloween characters including a cat, a witch and a ghoul, who are drawn to the tapping of a little girl's toe.

Van Rynbach, Iris. *Five Little Pumpkins.* Boyds Mills, 1995. The traditional finger rhyme is illustrated with lively watercolors.

Wyllie, Stephen. *Ghost Train: A Spooky Hologram Book.* Dial, 1992. Three ghosts search for a place to haunt before settling on the "Ghost Train" ride at an amusement park.

Ziefert, Harriet. *Two Little Witches: A Halloween Counting Story.* Candlewick, 1996. Two little witches meet a skeleton, a cat, a pirate and more on Halloween.

Ghost Wind Sock

Your storytime will be complete as you help the children make a ghost wind sock. This craft takes ten minutes to complete. You may wish to parade through the library with the children after storytime.

Directions

Cut 8½"x11" white paper in half to 4¼"x11. Cut four 12" strips of white crepe paper for each child. Use a single hole punch to punch two holes in the paper along long edge, as shown, and tie a 15" piece of string or yarn to the holes. This will be the handle. At storytime, allow the children to draw a face on the ghost. Let children tape four white crepe paper strips to the inside of the white paper along bottom edge. Tape or staple short ends of the paper together to create a tube.

This craft takes **10 minutes** to complete.

Hats

Before Sharing Books

Collect funny hats to display. Put them on stuffed animals around the room. Quiz the children about hats with questions like this. It is red, has a long bill in back, and protects the head from heat and falling objects. Whose hat is that? It is pointed and black. Whose hat is that? It is red with white fur around it, and it is long. Whose hat is that?

Rest Activities

Fingerplays and Action Rhymes

I Have Two Shoes

I have two shoes, two shoes, two shoes, *(touch your toes)*
I have two shoes, *(clap)* right here!

I have two mittens, two mittens, two mittens,
I have two mittens, *(clap)* right here! *(stand up straight)*

I have one hat, one hat, one hat,
I have one hat, *(clap)* right here! *(hands on head)*

Song

Jesse Parker Lost His Hat
Tune of: "Mary Had a Little Lamb"
Jesse Parker lost his hat,
Lost his hat, lost his hat.
Jesse Parker lost his hat,
And now his ears are cold.

Jesse found his mother's wig,
Mother's wig, mother's wig.
Jesse found his mother's wig,
The one with curls of gold.

Jesse Parker put it on,
Put it on, put it on.
Jesse Parker put it on,
So he could look his best.

Then the birdies chased him home,
Chased him home, chased him home.
Then the birdies chased him home,
It looked just like a nest.
[Adapted traditional song]

Books to Share

Dr. Suess. ***The 500 Hats of Bartholomew Cubbins.*** Random House, 1989. Bartholomew Cubbins appears to be defying the order of the Captain of the Guards by not removing his hat when the king goes by. Each time he removes his hat, another identical one appears on his head.

Gardella, Tricia. ***Casey's New Hat.*** Houghton Mifflin, 1997. Casey's hat is worn out, and despite searching all over the ranch and in town for a replacement, she can't find one that seems right until she sees Grandpa's stained, dusty, crumpled old hat.

Keller, Holly. ***Rosata.*** Greenwillow, 1995. Having found a hat with a bird on it, Camilla names the bird Rosata and takes the hat everywhere with her until she meets a new girl next door.

Marzollo, Jean. ***Ten Cats Have Hats.*** Scholastic, 1994. Pictures and rhyming text present animals from one bear to ten cats with their assorted possessions.

Slobodkina, Esphyr. ***Caps for Sale: A Tale of a Peddler.*** Harper & Row, 1985. The monkeys steal the peddler's caps while he is asleep.

Smath, Jerry. ***A Hat So Simple.*** Bridgewater, 1993. Edna the alligator has quite an adventure when she goes to buy a hat to wear while fishing with her husband Paul.

Stoeke, Janet Morgan. ***A Hat for Minerva Louise.*** Dutton, 1994. Minerva Louise, a snow-loving chicken, mistakes a pair of mittens for two hats to keep both ends warm.

Fancy Hats

Finish up your storytime by helping the children make a fancy hat. Then have a hat parade for the parents! This craft takes ten minutes to complete, since the children will probably get very creative with it.

Directions

Cut two 18" lengths of narrow ribbon for each child. Staple the ribbons to a paper plate as shown. Cut an assortment of paper shapes, such as flowers, squares, long strips for curling, butterflies, bats, birds, etc. Collect photos from magazines or newspapers, bits of ribbon, or any other small items. Let the children glue an assortment of decorations on their paper plate to make a fancy hat. Tie the ribbons under their chins and have a hat parade.

This craft takes **10 minutes** to complete.

Hippos

Before Sharing Books

Talk about where the children like to go when it is hot. Do they like to sit in the shade? Do they like to play in a swimming pool? Ask them if they would like to sit in a muddy puddle to cool off. That is where hippos cool off. Have them pretend that they are sitting in a muddy puddle to hear the stories about hippos.

Rest Activities

Fingerplays and Action Rhymes

Ten Little Hippos Full of Grace

Ten little hippos, full of grace,
Put a pleasant smile on their face,
And danced and danced all over the place! *(tiptoe around the room)*
But they smashed all the furniture.
What a *disgrace! (fall to the ground)*

Hot Hippo

I'm a hippo,
Hot, hot, hot. *(fan face with hand)*
I'm going to my favorite spot. *(walk slowly)*
Down to the mudhole,
Squish, squish, squish. *(wiggle down to a squat)*
Where I can get cool,
As cool as I wish. *Ahhh!*

Song

Ten Little Hippos Fat
Tune of: "Ten Little Indians"
One little, two little, three little hippos.
Four little, five little, six little hippos.
Seven little, eight little, nine little hippos.
Ten little hippos *FAT!*
[Adapted traditional song]

Books to Share

Boynton, Sandra. ***Hippos Go Berserk.*** Simon & Schuster, 1997. Larger and larger groups of hippos join a lone hippo for a night-time party.

Flanders, Michael. ***The Hippopotamus Song: A Muddy Love Story.*** Little, Brown, 1991. Lovestruck hippos and their muddy escapades provide inspiration for a humorous song. Musical notation included.

McCarthy, Bobette. ***Happy Hiding Hippos.*** Bradbury, 1993. Jolly hippos play a rambunctious game of hide-and-seek all over town.

————. ***Ten Little Hippos.*** Bradbury, 1992. The mishaps of a troupe of dancing hippos give the reader the opportunity to count down from ten to one.

Minarik, Else **Holmelund. *Am I Beautiful?*** Greenwillow, 1992. Overhearing other mothers call their children beautiful, a young hippo tries to find out if he is beautiful as well.

Mwenye Hadithi. ***Hot Hippo.*** Little, Brown, 1986. Hippo asks permission from Ngai to live in the water, promising not to eat the little fishes.

Standing Hippo

Finish up your day in the mud by making a hippo that can stand up.

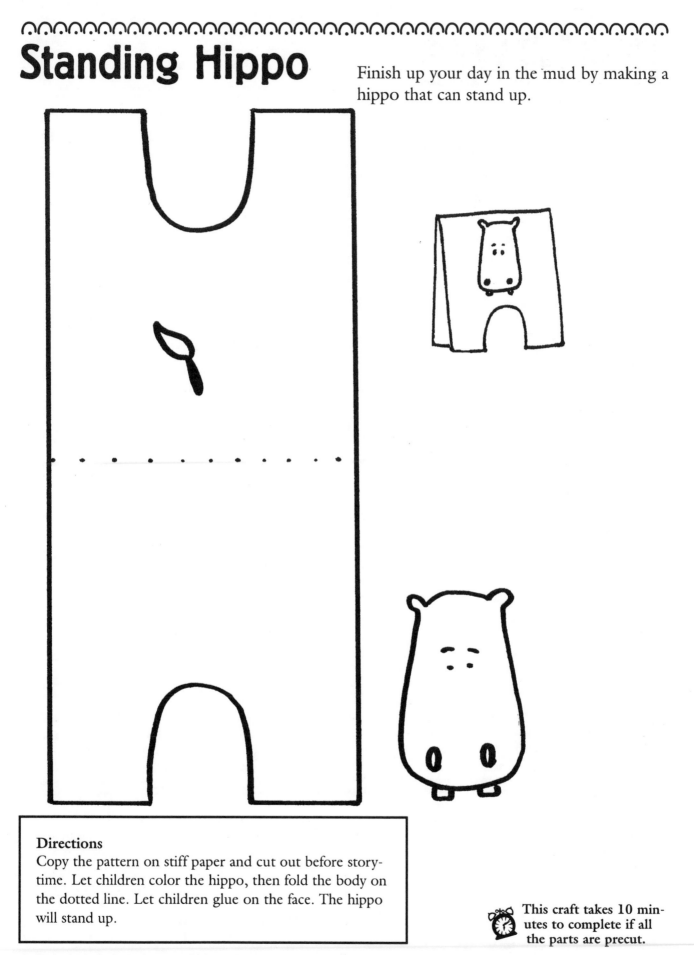

Directions
Copy the pattern on stiff paper and cut out before story-time. Let children color the hippo, then fold the body on the dotted line. Let children glue on the face. The hippo will stand up.

This craft takes 10 minutes to complete if all the parts are precut.

Ireland

Before Sharing Books

Play a recording of Irish folk music as the children are coming in. Be sure to wear something green. Tell the children you are going to take them on a trip to the Emerald Isle. This is a beautiful land where the ocean breezes feel fresh and the turf is very green. In this country little boys are called "laddies" and little girls are called "lassies". Many people grow potatoes, and many people believe in magic little people called leprechauns. When all the laddies and lassies are ready, begin.

Rest Activities

Fingerplays and Action Rhymes

Lazy Leprechaun

A lazy leprechaun took a nap, *(lay head on hands)*
Under a shady tree. *(arms up high)*
I tiptoed, tiptoed up to him, *(walk on tiptoes)*
And caught that leprechaun by the chin. *(grab at air)*
At first he scowled, *(eyebrows down, pouting mouth)*
And then he grinned, *(smile)*
And gave his gold to me. *(point to self)*

Green Are the Hills

Green are the hills as I walk by, *(draw imaginary hills)*
Green are the trees that reach the sky, *(arms up high)*
Green are the shamrocks, *(pretend to hold a
   shamrock in your fingers)*
Green are my eyes. *(point to eyes)*
I'm an Irish Lassie (or Laddie). *It's no surprise!*
   (point to self)

Game

One Potato

Everyone holds out their fists. Leader goes around the room and strikes each fist with her own saying:

One potato, two potato, three potato, four.
Five potato, six potato, seven potato, more.

On the word more, the child places that fist behind his back. Continue until all fists are gone. Owner of the last fist remaining is the winner.
[Traditional game]

Books to Share

Bateman, Teresa. *The Ring of Truth: An Original Irish Tale.* Holiday House, 1997. After the king of the leprechauns gives him the Ring of Truth, Patrick O'Kelley no longer expects to win a blarney contest.

Bunting, Eve. *Market Day.* HarperCollins, 1996. Tess and Wee Boy visit the farm animals, wonder at the sword-swallower, listen to the playing pipes, and experience all the excitement of a country fair in Ireland.

DePaola, Tomie. *Fin M'Coul: The Giant of Knockmany Hill.* Holiday House, 1981. Fin M'Coul's wife, Oonagh, helps him outwit his rival, Cucullin. Also: *Jamie O'Rourke and the Big Potato: An Irish Folktale.*

Greene, Ellin. *Billy Beg and His Bull: An Irish Tale.* Holiday House, 1994. With magical gifts from the bull his mother had given him, the son of an Irish king manages to prove his bravery and win a princess as his wife.

Nimmo, Jenny. *The Starlight Cloak.* Dial, 1993. An Irish princess leads a life of misery until her foster mother reveals magical powers that change her life forever.

Shute, Linda. *Clever Tom and the Leprechaun: An Old Irish Story.* Lothrop Lee & Shepard, 1988. Clever Tom Fitzpatrick thinks his fortune is made when he captures a leprechaun and forces him to reveal the hiding place of his gold, but the leprechaun is clever, too.

Lucky Shamrock

After your stories, help the children make a lucky shamrock to take home.

Directions

Using the pattern, cut three green hearts for each child. Let the children glue the points together with a glue stick. Staple or tape a green pipe cleaner to the back of the shamrock as shown, to make the stem.

 This craft takes 5 minutes to complete.

Korea

Before Sharing Books

Ask the children to think of something that keeps them safe. They might suggest parents, seat belts, dog, etc. Ask them if they sleep with a special blanket or teddy bear. Does it make them feel safe at night? Everyone wants to feel safe. Long ago, the people of Korea believed that the blue dragon would protect them from the east, and the white tiger would protect them from the west. Images of dragons and tigers can be found on many buildings in Korea today.

Rest Activities

Fingerplays and Action Rhymes

Two Brothers

Two brothers sat on the garden wall. *(hold up index fingers on each hand)*

One was big and the other was small. *(wiggle one finger, then the other)*

Big brother ran away to play. *(one hand behind back)*

Little brother followed him anyway. *(other hand behind back)*

Soon they came back and I heard them say, *(both hands in front)*

"Let's play together for the rest of the day!" *(put hands close together and cross fingers)*

To Market

To market, to market, to buy a fat pig.
Home again, home again, jiggedy jig.
To market, to market, to buy a fat hog.
Home again, home again, joggedy jog.
To market, to market, a story to buy.
Home again, home again, happy am I.
[Adapted traditional rhyme]

Clap hands on the beat.

Game

Cinderella Dressed in Yella

Cinderella, dressed in yella,
Went upstairs to kiss a fella.
Made a mistake.
Kissed a snake.
How many doctors did it take?
[Traditional rhyme]

A child jumps a rope until she misses, and this is the number of doctors. You may choose instead to select a number for the group to count up to, clapping as you count.

Books to Share

Climo, Shirley. *The Korean Cinderella.* HarperCollins, 1993. Pear Blossom, a stepchild, eventually comes to be chosen by the magistrate for his wife.

Farley, Carol. *Mr. Pak Buys a Story.* Whitman, 1997. A wealthy couple send their servant out to buy a very good story that will entertain them in the evenings. The unusual story that the servant buys from a thief proves to be well worth the price.

Jaffe, Nina. *Older Brother, Younger Brother: A Korean Folktale.* Viking, 1995. After being turned out by his greedy brother, Hungbu and his family become very rich when his kindness to an injured sparrow is rewarded. Hungbu then shares his wealth with his brother's family.

O'Brien, Ann Sibley. *The Princess and the Beggar: A Korean Folktale.* Scholastic, 1992. A sad princess finally discovers happiness after marrying a beggar.

Rhee, Nami. *Magic Spring: A Korean Folktale.* Putnam, 1993. An old man and his wife discover a fountain of youth. They drink from it and become young again. The only thing in the world they still want is a child. When a greedy neighbor drinks from the spring, the results are surprising.

Korean Blue Dragon

Finish your storytime by helping the children make a blue dragon, which can protect them from the east.

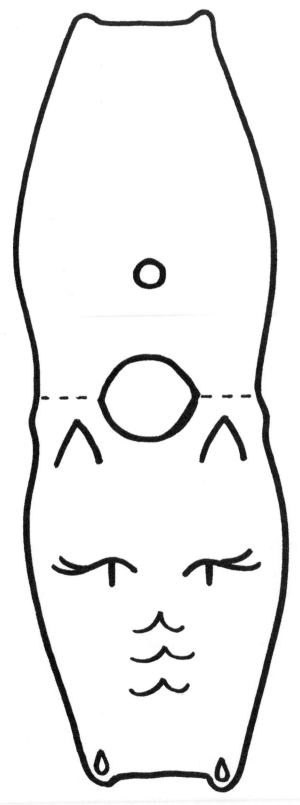

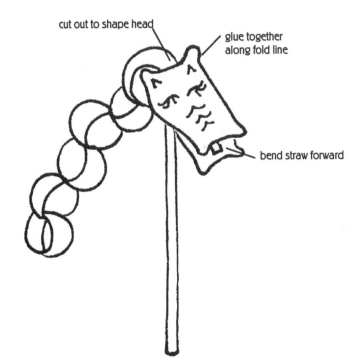

cut out to shape head

glue together along fold line

bend straw forward

Directions

Copy and cut out dragon head on blue paper for each child. Cut out the large circle along the fold line to shape the dragon head. Insert a flexible drinking straw in small hole on lower jaw and tape it in place. Fold head over, so straw is inside dragon's head. Glue dragon head near fold line closed. Bend straw forward towards the front of the mouth. Cut strips of blue paper 1"x 8½". Let the children make paper chains from the blue strips. Tape the paper chain to the straw, near the head. Let the children hold the straw and walk with their dragons in a parade around the room.

 This craft takes 10 minutes to complete if all the parts are precut.

Mexico

Before Sharing Books

If they are available to you, display a piñata, a sombrero, a Mexican blanket, pottery, jewelry or other arts and crafts. Cut out some red chile peppers from bright paper and hang them on a string in a bunch, or hang real chile peppers. Display puppets or dolls of coyote, rabbit and sheep. Teach the children how to say good morning in Spanish. "Buenos dias." Invite them to Mexico with you for a short vacation and some great stories.

Rest Activities

Fingerplays and Action Rhymes

Colors

Blue is azul [uh-SÜL] like the sky up there. *(reach up)*

Negro [NAY-grō] is black like the shoes I wear. *(touch shoes)*

Verde [VĀR-day] is green like the leafy trees. *(wave hands high)*

Rosa [RŌ-suh] is pink like my rosy knees. *(touch knees)*

Cafe [KAH-fay] is brown like a brown toad stool. *(squat down low)*

Blanco [BLŎN-cō] is white like the snow so cool. *(wiggle fingers like snowflakes)*

Little Mouse

Here comes a little mouse.
El raton. [el ra-TŌN] *(make fingers creep up arm)*
Va a casa. [Băh ăh KĂH-săh]
Run back home!

Run in a circle, come back to your original place.

Counting

Uno, dos, tres. [OO-nō, dōs, trās]
One, two three.
Count in Spanish!
Count with me!

Four, five, six.
Cuatro, cinco, seis. [KWAH-trō, SINK-ō, SĀS]
When I count in Spanish,
I wear a happy face.

Books to Share

Aardema, Verra. *Borreguita and the Coyote: A Tale from Ayutla, Mexico.* Knopf, 1991. A little lamb uses her clever wiles to keep coyote from eating her up.

————. *Pedro and the Padre: A Tale from Jalisco, Mexico.* Dial, 1991. A lazy boy learns a lesson about lying.

Ada, Alma Flor *Mediapollito/ Half Chicken: A New Version of a Traditional Story.* Doubleday, 1995. A Mexican folktale which explains why the weather vane has a little rooster on one end that spins around to let us know which way the wind is blowing.

Climo, Shirley. *The Little Red Ant and the Great Big Crumb: A Mexican Fable.* Clarion, 1995. A small red ant finds a crumb in a Mexican corn field, but she does not believe she is strong enough to carry it, so she goes off to find someone who is.

DePaola, Tomie. *The Legend of the Poinsettia.* Putnam, 1994. When Lucida cannot finish her gift for the Baby Jesus in time for the Christmas procession, a miracle enables her to offer the beautiful flower we now call the poinsettia.

Johnston, Tony. *The Tale of Rabbit and Coyote.* Putnam, 1994. Rabbit outwits Coyote in the Zapotec tale which explains why coyotes howl at the moon.

Ojos de Dios
Eyes of God

After your stories help the children make a Mexican decoration. Ojos de Dios can be worn around the neck as a good luck ornament. Two ways to make it are shown. The simple version is best for young children. This version takes five minutes, if all parts are precut. You may wish to make the traditional version to show the children.

Simplified method

Cut diamonds in all three sizes using different colors for each.

Traditional method

Wrap colored yarn around craft sticks to form pattern as shown.

Directions

Simplified method: Cut diamond shapes from paper or felt in three sizes using the pattern above. Use several bright colors, especially primary colors. Punch a hole in one end of the largest diamond and tie a 24" piece of string through it. Let the children glue the smaller diamonds centered inside the larger ones as shown in the illustration. Let them wear it around their neck.

Traditional method: Tie two craft sticks together to form a cross. Wrap colored yarn around each stick, continuing around for several complete rows. Tie another color to the end of the yarn and continue wrapping for a few rows. Tie a third color to the end of the yarn and wrap until you are nearly at the edge of the craft sticks. Tie the end securely to the craft stick. Tie a 24" piece of yarn to one end, so the charm can be worn around the neck. It also can be hung in a window of your house for good luck.

 This craft takes 5 minutes to complete if all parts are precut.

Mice

Before Sharing Books

Ask the children to name some very small animals. When they have mentioned mice, ask them if they can be very small, like a mouse. Allow them to crawl under a chair or table which is the door to your mouse house, and tell them the stories today will be read inside the mouse house.

Rest Activities

Fingerplays and Action Rhymes

Five Little Mice

Five little mice on the pantry floor, *(hold up five fingers)*

This little mouse peeked behind the door. *(cup hands around face)*

This little mouse nibbled at the cake. *(pretend to eat)*

This little mouse not a sound did make. *(hold finger in front of mouth, shh…)*

This little mouse took a bite of cheese. *(pretend to eat)*

This little mouse heard the kitten sneeze. *(cup hand around ear)*

"Ah choo!" sneezed the kitten,

and "Squeak!" they cried. *(hold hands up as if surprised)*

As they found a hole and ran inside. *(run in place)*

[Traditional]

Where Are the Baby Mice?

Where are the baby mice? Squeak, squeak, squeak. *(hands behind back)*

I cannot see them. Peek, peek, peek. *(hold hand over eyes as if looking)*

Here they come from the hole in the wall. *(bring out one hand, held in a fist)*

One, two, thee, four, five—that's all. *(bring fingers out of fist one at a time)*

[Traditional]

Songs

Hickory, Dickory, Dock

Hickory, Dickory, Dock.
The mouse ran up the clock.
The clock struck one, the mouse ran down.
Hickory, Dickory, Dock.
[Traditional]

Three Blind Mice

Three blind mice. Three blind mice.
See how they run. See how the run.
They all ran up to the farmer's wife.
She cut off their tails with a carving knife.
Did you ever see such a sight in your life,
As three blind mice?
[Traditional]

Books to Share

Kraus, Robert. *Come Out and Play, Little Mouse.* Greenwillow, 1987. Little mouse is busy helping his family five days of the week, but he still gets to play on the weekends.

McMillan, Bruce. *Mouse Views.* Holiday House, 1993. An escaped pet mouse runs through school, showing objects such as scissors, paper, books, and chalk from a mouse's point of view.

Numeroff, Laura Joffe. *If You Give a Mouse a Cookie.* Haper & Row, 1985. Relating the cycle of requests a mouse is likely to make after you give him a cookie takes the reader through a young child's day.

Waddell, Martin. *Squeak-a-lot.* Greenwillow, 1991. A mouse searches for a playmate and hears a variety of animal sounds.

Walsh, Ellen Stoll. *Mouse Paint.* Harcourt Brace Jovanovich, 1989. Three white mice discover jars of red, blue and yellow paint with which they explore the world of color.

Wood, Don and Audrey. *The Little Mouse, the Red Ripe Strawberry and the Big Hungry Bear.* Child's Play, 1995. A mouse picks a red, ripe strawberry and must hide it from the big, hungry bear.

Mouse Puppet

Finish your mice storytime by making a mouse puppet.

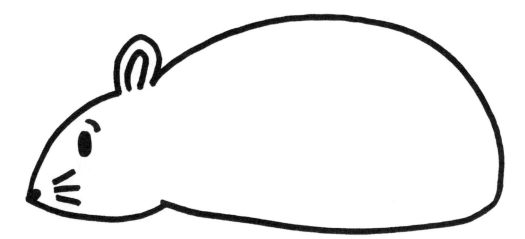

Directions

Copy mouse on stiff paper and cut out before storytime. Cut rug yarn into ½" and 4" pieces before storytime. You will need one 4" piece and many ½" pieces for each puppet. Let the children glue ½" pieces of yarn on the mouse to make him furry. Let them glue on a 4" tail. Glue the mouse onto a craft stick to make a puppet.

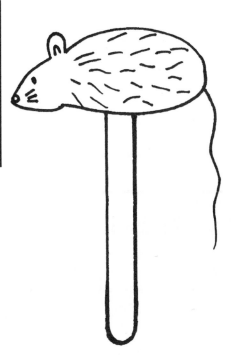

 This craft takes **10** minutes to complete if the mice are precut.

Monkeys

Before Sharing Books

Get in the mood for some monkey business by having the children sing "This Is the Way." Pantomime peeling a banana, swinging in a tree, and other monkey tricks.

Rest Activities

Songs

This Is the Way
This is the way we peel a banana,
peel a banana, peel a banana.
This is the way we peel a banana,
so early in the morning.
[Adapted traditional song]

Pop! Goes the Weasel
All around the cobbler's bench,
The monkey chased the weasel.
The monkey thought it all in fun.
Pop! Goes the weasel.

A penny for a spool of thread,
A penny for a needle.
That's the way the money goes.
Pop! Goes the weasel.
[Traditional]

Game

Monkey See, Monkey Do
The first time through, the leader should be the storyteller. Children may take a turn as leader once the game is understood by all. Leader says, "Monkey see, monkey do." Leader performs an action for the children to imitate, such as touching the head, standing on one foot, hopping, etc. The leader then changes to another action. At first, the leader gives plenty of time for the children to imitate the action, but soon the leader changes from one action to the next more quickly. The speed increases until the game becomes so funny that the "little monkeys" can no longer imitate the actions. A new leader may then be chosen and the game repeated, as time permits.
[Traditional]

Books to Share

Christelow, Eileen. *Five Little Monkeys Jumping on the Bed*. Clarion, 1989. One by one, the monkeys jump on the bed and fall off and bump their heads.

Ho, Minfong. *Hush! : A Thai Lullaby*. Orchard, 1996. This lullaby book asks animals such as a lizard, a monkey and a water-buffalo to be quiet and not disturb a sleeping baby.

Lake, Mary Dixon. *The Royal Drum: An Ashanti Tale*. Mondo, 1996. All the animals, except lazy monkey, work to make a drum for the King of the Jungle, but Ananzi sees to it that he gets the hardest job of all.

Myers, Walter Dean. *How Mr. Monkey Saw the Whole World*. Doubleday, 1996. Mr. Buzzard avoids working for his food by tricking other animals, but Mr. Monkey finds a way to remedy the situation.

San Souci, Robert. *Pedro and the Monkey*. Morrow, 1996. A monkey secures the fortune of his owner in this variation of a folktale from the Philippines.

Slobodkina, Esphyr. *Caps for Sale*. Harper & Row, 1985. A peddler selling caps falls asleep under a tree full of monkeys and wakes to find his caps are missing.

Swinging Monkey

Finish up your monkey business by helping the children make a swinging monkey. This craft takes five minutes to complete. Allow time to play with them.

Directions

Copy and cut out the monkeys. Fold on dotted line. Punch holes in both of the hands. Let the children color the monkeys. Put a straw through the punched holes and twirl.

 This craft takes 10 minutes to complete.

Monsters

Before Sharing Books

Teach the children the "Go, Monster, Go" rhyme. Be sure your storytime room has no monsters in it by repeating the rhyme and chasing them away from the table, the chairs, the closet or anywhere else they might hide. When you are safe, you may begin reading your monster stories.

Rest Activities

Fingerplays and Action Rhymes

Five Little Monsters

Five little monsters looking for a meal. *(hold up five fingers)*
One ate a rotten orange peel. *(pretend to pop these foods into mouth)*

One ate a moldy piece of bread.
One ate a glob of glue instead.

One ate a bowl of bat wing jelly.
One at a tennis shoe, old and smelly.

After their lunch, they gave a clap. *(clap hands)*
Hung upside down, *(bend down from the waste and let hands hang)*
And took a nap. *(snore loudly)*

Go, Monster, Go

Monster, monster under the bed, *(chair, etc.)*
   (cup hands around mouth)
You should go somewhere else instead! *(shake finger)*
Go, monster, go! *(stamp feet slowly)*
Go, monster, go! *(stamp feet faster)*
Go, monster, go! *(stamp feet very fast)*

Game

Monster Mash

Play some scary music. Turn your back on the group and let them dance and walk like monsters. When you turn off the music and turn around to face them, they must freeze. If they are still moving, they must sit up front with you. Continue until there are no more monsters, or until you are tired of the game.

Books to Share

Auch, Mary Jane. ***Monster Brother.*** Holiday House, 1994. Rodney is relieved to find out that his new baby brother's cries are loud enough to frighten any monster away from their bedroom.

Baron, Alan. ***The Red Fox Monster.*** Candlewick, 1996. Someone is hiding in the bushes. Is it Red Fox, or Dan Dog, or Tabby Cat dressed up in Red Fox's clothes?

Emberly, Ed. ***Go Away, Big Green Monster!*** Little, Brown, 1992. Die-cut pages reveal bits of monster and are designed to help a child control nighttime fears of monsters.

Euvremer, Teryl. ***Tripple Whammy.*** HarperCollins, 1993. A monster and a witch grow bored with their marriage when they run out of ways to be mean to each other, until they transform themselves into various interesting creatures.

Hutchins, Pat. ***Three-Star Billy.*** Greenwillow, 1994. Billy, a bad-tempered little monster who does not want to be in nursery school, throws tantrums that only result in his teacher giving him praise and three stars.

Kasza, Keiko. ***Grandpa Toad's Secrets.*** Putnam, 1995. Grandpa Toad teaches his grandson the secrets of survival, but Little Toad is the one who saves the day when a huge monster attacks them.

Rosenberg, Liz. ***Monster Mama.*** Philomel, 1993. Patrick Edward's fierce monster mother helps him deal with some obnoxious bullies

Sendak, Maurice. ***Where the Wild Things Are.*** Harper & Row, 1963. A little boy is sent to bed without his supper, then sails to the land of the wild things where he becomes their king.

Monster Feet

Finish up your monster stories by helping the children make monster feet, which they will wear on their hands. This craft takes ten minutes to complete, and will make monsters out of the whole bunch!

Directions

Trace the monster feet onto heavy paper, making two for each child. Allow the children to color the toes with crayons and glue on colored spots to create their personalized monster feet. Fasten the monster feet around their wrists with tape, paperclips or staples.

 This craft takes **10 minutes** to complete.

Moose

Before Sharing Books

Make a set of moose antlers to wear on your head while you read the stories. Take a walk with the children to the far north, using giant moose steps. When you have arrived at a good place for stories, sit everyone down.

Rest Activities

Fingerplays and Action Rhymes

Kidstuff 6:8 and *Copy Cat* Jan/Feb 1993 have good moose activities. Also try these:

Mr. Moose

Mr. Moose is very tall. *(stand tall)*
His antlers touch the sky. *(reach hands up)*
They make a real good resting place,
For birdies passing by. *(make hands talk like birdies)*

Steps

I can take giant moose steps. *(step in place)*
I can take tiny mouse steps. *(tiptoe in place)*
I can take quick, quick bunny hops. *(hop in place)*
I can sit still, as still as a rock. *(sit down)*

Poem

Moose Pride

If I were a moose I'd be proud of my nose,
As big as a house and as long as a hose.
I'd smell every raindrop, or pine tree, or rose.
I would be so happy, I'd dance on my toes.

If I were a moose I'd be proud to stand tall.
I'd walk through deep rivers, no problem at all.
My legs could step over dead trees where they fall.
I'd see all around me because I'd be tall.

If I were a moose I'd be proud of my head,
With antlers that spread out as wide as a shed,
A perch for the birdies, brown, yellow and red.
I'd be proud of the antlers on top of my head.

Books to Share

Alexander, Martha. *Even That Moose Won't Listen to Me.* Dial, 1988. A little girl tries various means to get rid of a moose in the garden after she repeatedly tells her family the moose is there and they do not believe her.

Balan, Bruce. *The Moose in the Dress.* Clarkson Potter, 1991. A little boy cannot sleep when he sees a shadow on his bedroom wall.

Numeroff, Laura Joffe. *If You Give a Moose a Muffin.* HarperCollins, 1991. Chaos can ensue if you give a moose a muffin and start him on a cycle of urgent requests.

Small, David. *Imogene's Antlers.* Crown, 1985. One Thursday Imogene wakes up with a pair of antlers growing out of her head and causes a sensation wherever she goes.

Stapler, Sarah. *Spruce the Moose Cuts Loose.* Putnam, 1992. Spruce the Moose's enormous antlers cause him all sorts of problems in his daily life.

Wiseman, Bernard. *Morris Tells Boris Mother Moose Stories and Rhymes.* Dodd, Mead, 1979. In order to help Boris the Bear fall asleep, Morris the Moose tells his friend some very familiar stories.

Moose Antler
Headbands

Finish your story time by helping the children make a set of antlers to wear.

Directions
Cut a headband from construction paper for each child, 1"x 18". Using the pattern, cut out a set antlers for each child. Allow the children to color antlers. Tape the tab to the headband. Adjust the headband to fit child and tape the ends together.

This craft takes 5 minutes to complete if the parts are precut.

Mothers

Before Sharing Books

You may wish to invite the mothers to come to storytime today, and provide a light refreshment for them as a treat. Set up a display of mother and baby stuffed animals beside your books. Introduce the mothers by asking the children to raise their hand if their mother likes to sing, is a good cook, has brown eyes, grows house plants, etc.

Rest Activities

Fingerplays and Actions Rhymes

Right Here in My Pocket

Right here in my pocket, *(point to shirt pocket)*
Is a big surprise for you. *(point away from self)*
It isn't an umbrella, *(cover index finger with palm of other hand)*
Or a monster who says *"Boo."* *(raise hands like claws and say Boo)*
It's not a wiggly spider, *(make fingers wiggle)*
Or a snake who likes to hiss. *(slither arm like a snake)*
Right here in my pocket, *(point to shirt pocket)*
Is a big, two-handed kiss.
MMMMMMMMM-Whah! *(throw a kiss)*
[Traditional]

Song

Did You Ever See a Mommy
Tune of: "Did You Ever See a Lassy"
Did you ever see a Mommy, a Mommy, a Mommy.
Did you ever see a Mommy, go this way and that?
Go this way and that way, and this way and that way.
Did you ever see a Mommy go this way and that?

Actions to use: rocking a baby, sweeping the floor, stirring a cake mix.

Game

Mother May I?
Children line up with their backs against a wall. Leader stands across the room with her back against the wall. Leader calls out an action for the children to do, such as take one giant step forward, take one bunny hop forward, take three mouse steps backward, etc. Before they can take the step, they must ask, "Mother, may I?" The leader responds, "Yes, you may." If the child does not ask, he may not take the steps. (With very young children this rule will not be stressed.). When at least one child reaches the wall where the leader is standing, the game is over.

I ♥ MOM

Books to Share

Asch, Frank. **Bread and Honey.** Parents Magazine Press, 1981. Ben paints a picture of his mother, with help from Owl, Rabbit, Alligator, Elephant, Lion and Giraffe.

Balian, Lorna. **Mother's Mother's Day.** Abingdon, 1982. Hazel the mouse goes to visit her mother on Mother's Day, but finds she has gone to visit her mother.

Guarino, Deborah. **Is Your Mama a Llama?** Scholastic, 1989. A young llama asks his friends if their mamas are llamas and finds out, in rhyme, that their mothers are other types of animals.

Kasza, Keiko. **A Mother for Choco.** Putnam, 1992. A lonely little bird goes in search of a mother.

Russo, Marisabina. **Trade-in Mother.** Greenwillow, 1993. Max discusses with his mother good reasons why he would like to trade her in, but admits there is one reason to keep her.

Waddell, Martin. **Owl Babies.** Candlewick, 1992. Three owl babies try to stay calm while their mother is gone.

Mother's Day Kisses

Make this sweet Mother's Day card at the end of your storytime.

Directions

Using the pattern, cut out "kisses" from pink construction paper. Each child will need five or six "kisses." Copy the poem and cut out for each child. Fold a white sheet of construction paper in half for each child. Let the children paste the verse and several kisses on the card. Children may write their name or color on the card if desired.

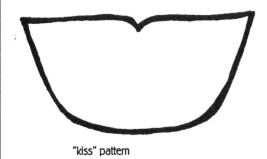

"kiss" pattern

MOTHER'S DAY KISSES

I LOVE YOU, MOMMY,
SO HERE'S WHAT I'LL DO.
I'LL GIVE YOU KISSES ALL THE DAY
THROUGH.
LET'S COUNT THE KISSES.
IT'S NOT VERY HARD.
THEN I'LL GIVE YOU REAL ONES
ALONG WITH THIS CARD.

 This craft takes 10 minutes to complete.

Native Americans

Before Sharing Books

Build a cold campfire from logs in the center of your storytime area. Seat the children around the campfire. Tell them you are going to read stories today from several tribes of American Indians. Show art, clothing or jewelry from a local tribe. Tell the children that tribes from other areas had different kinds of houses, spoke different languages, and made their clothing in different ways. Tell them that stories are special to American Indians. Usually the grandparents would tell the stories to the children on winter nights.

Rest Activities

Fingerplays and Action Rhymes

Hiding Game

I'm hiding a ball where you can't see. *(cup hands to form a ball)*

Is it under the blanket? *(spread palms down like a blanket)*

Is it near a tall tree? *(reach high)*

Is it in a cooking pot? *(arms in a circle as if holding a pot)*

Try to find it,

Then you can be the next to hide it.

Guessing games are common among all tribes. A peach pit, a stone, or a ball made of leather could be used for the guessing game.

Song

Hush-a-Bye

Hush-a-bye,

Don't you cry.

Go to sleep little baby.

When you wake, you shall have,

All the pretty little horses.

Dapples and grays,

Pintos and bays.

All the pretty little horses.

[Traditional song]

To the plains indians, a fast horse was a very valuable possession.

Books to Share

Bierhorst, John. *The Woman Who Fell From the Sky: The Iroquois Story of Creation*. Morrow, 1993. A woman fell down to earth from sky country, and the earth's creation was completed by her two sons.

Bruchac, Joseph. *The First Strawberries: A Cherokee Story*. Dial, 1993. A quarrel between first man and first woman is reconciled when the Sun causes strawberries to grow out of the earth.

Hillerman, Tony. *The Boy Who Made Dragonfly: A Zuni Myth*. University of New Mexico Press, 1993. A young boy and his sister gain the wisdom from the dragonfly that makes them leaders of their people.

Martin, Rafe. *The Boy Who Lived With the Seals*. Putnam, 1993. A lost boy who has grown up in the sea with seals returns to his tribe in this Chinook legend.

———. *Rough -Faced Girl*. Putnam, 1992. An Algonquin version of the Cinderella story. The rough-faced girl and her two beautiful sisters compete for the love of the Invisible Being.

Taylor, Harriet Peck. *Coyote Places the Stars*. Bradbury, 1993. Coyote arranges the stars in the shape of his animal friends in this legend from the Wasco Indians.

Stevens, Janet. *Coyote Steals the Blanket: A Ute Tale*. Holiday House, 1993. Coyote gets what's coming to him when he takes something that does not belong to him.

Young, Ed. *Moon Mother: A Native American Creation Tale*. HarperCollins, 1993. The Creator Spirit falls in love with a Woman Spirit who becomes the moon he carries through the sky every night. The tribe is unspecified.

Feather Headband

After your stories are finished, let the children decorate a feather for a headband. Explain that a feather is given as an honor to someone who has been very brave.

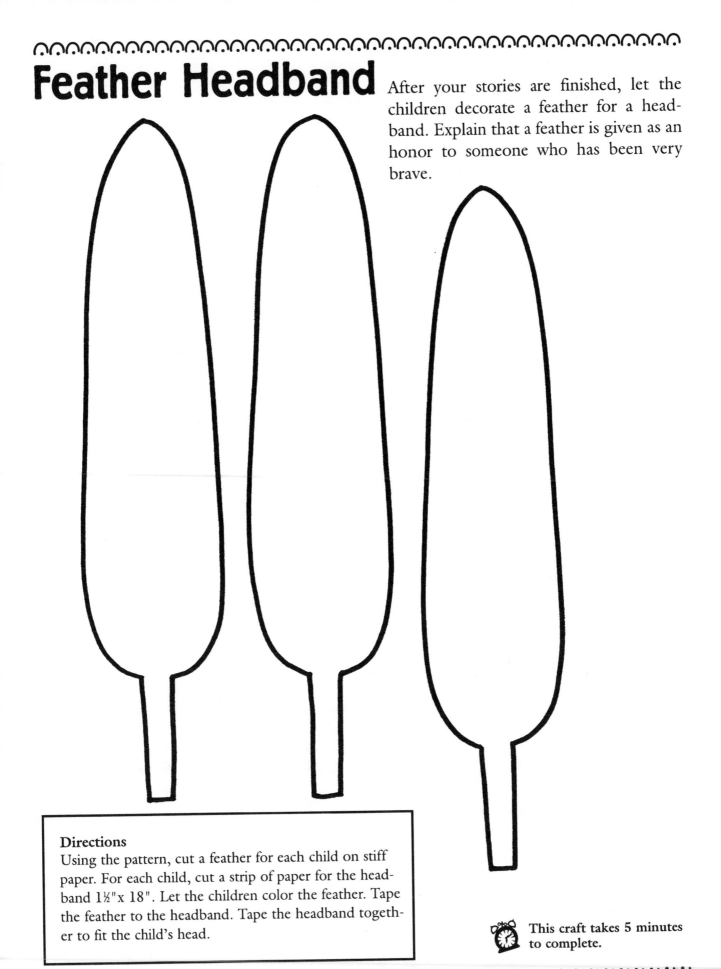

Directions

Using the pattern, cut a feather for each child on stiff paper. For each child, cut a strip of paper for the headband 1½"x 18". Let the children color the feather. Tape the feather to the headband. Tape the headband together to fit the child's head.

This craft takes 5 minutes to complete.

Night

Before Sharing Books

Invite children to come in their pajamas to this storytime. Quilts and pillows could be spread around the room. Sing a lullaby and teach it to the group.

Rest Activities

Fingerplays and Action Rhymes

Sleep Tight

Little lambs have all come home. *(make a tail with one hand)*

Good night. Good night. *(rest face on hands)*

Little birds are in their nests. *(make hands "talk")*

Sleep tight. Sleep tight. *(rest face on hands)*

Little one, I'll tuck you in. *(pull the blanket to your chin, cup hands around chin)*

Good night. Good night.

Sleep tight. Sleep tight. *(rest face on hands)*

Bye Baby Bunting

Bye baby bunting, *(wave bye-bye)*

Daddy's gone a-hunting, *(pretend to ride a horse)*

To get a little rabbit skin, *(roll arms as if wrapping)*

To wrap his baby bunting in. *(pretend to rock a baby in arms)*

[Traditional rhyme]

Song

All My Fingers Go to Sleep

Tune of: "London Bridge"

All my fingers go to sleep, *(open hands wide)*

Go to sleep, go to sleep. *(slowly curl fingers into a fist)*

All my fingers go to sleep.

Wake up! *(quickly open hands again)*

[Traditional song]

Books to Share

Bandes, Hanna. *Sleepy River.* Philomel, 1993. A canoe ride at dusk provides a mother and child glimpses of ducks, fireflies, bats and other wonders of nature.

Christelow, Eileen. *The Five-Dog Night.* Clarion, 1993. Ezra keeps rebuffing his neighbor Old Betty when she tries to tell him how to survive the cold winter nights.

DeFelice, Cynthia. *Willy's Silly Grandma.* Orchard, 1997. Willy doesn't believe in any of his grandmother's superstitions, until he ventures down by the Big Swamp one dark night and comes to realize how smart Grandma is.

Hayes, Sarah. *This Is the Bear and the Scary Night.* Joy Street, 1992. A stuffed bear left behind in the park has an exciting night and is found safe the next morning in the spot where he was left.

London, Jonathan. *The Owl Who Became the Moon.* Dutton, 1993. While riding on a train at night, a young boy listens and watches as he passes by many creatures in their wilderness homes.

Roennfeldt, Mary. *What's That Noise?* Orchard, 1992. A zookeeper hears a strange noise at night and searches in vain for its origin.

Watson, Wendy. *Fox Went Out On a Chilly Night.* Lothrop Lee & Shepard, 1994. An illustrated version of the folk song in which fox travels many miles to get dinner for his family.

Wickstrom, Thor. *The Big Night Out.* Dial, 1993. Bear, Mouse and Goose go out for a night on the town.

Sleepy Face

Finish your nighttime stories by making a sleepy face.

Directions

Copy the face pattern for each child and cut out. Put all the parts in a small envelope or baggie for each child. Let the children paste the sleepy eyes, nose and mouth on one side of the face. Let them paste the awake eyes, nose and mouth on the other side. Sing a lullaby and let the children turn the face from awake to asleep as you sing.

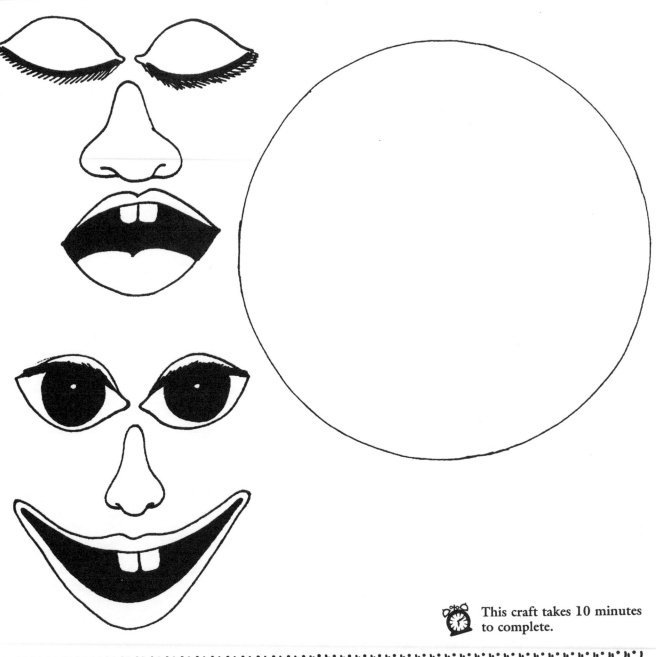

This craft takes **10 minutes to complete.**

Penguins

Before Sharing Books

Dress yourself (or a puppet) in a scarf, hat, mittens, coat and other warm clothing as you tell the children you are getting ready to go to a very cold place for storytime. Tell them you are going to read stories about birds that live on the ice and swim in the cold ocean. Settle everyone on an imaginary iceberg of their own, then begin your stories.

Rest Activities

Fingerplays and Action Rhymes

Penguin Cheer

I like fishies. Yes I do.
When I want fishies, here's what I do.
One, two, three…Splash! (*jump forward, arms overhead*)

Two Little Penguins

Two little penguins sitting on the ice. (*hold up index finger*)
One bows once, the other bows twice. (*make fingers bow*)
Waddle little penguins. Waddle away. (*put fingers behind back.*)
Come back penguins. Time to play. (*bring them to the front*)

Baby Penguins

One baby penguin makes a wish. (*hold up one finger, point to the stars*)
Two baby penguins catch a fish. (*hold up two fingers, clap hands together*)
Three baby penguins slip and slide. (*hold up three fingers, slide feet*)
Four baby penguins run and hide. (*hold up four fingers, run in place*)
Five baby penguins look around
Calling, "Mamma! Mamma! Mamma!" (*hold up five fingers, hand above eyebrows*)
Now they are found. (*hug arms around self*)

Books to Share

Alborough, Jez. *Cuddly Dudley.* Candlewick, 1993. Tired of being cuddled by his family, Dudley Penguin waddles away from home and encounteres something even worse than an affectionate family.

Benson, Patrick. *Little Penguin.* Philomel, 1991. Comparing herself to the larger Emperor Penguins, Pip the Adelie Penguin feels unhappy with her size until an encounter with a huge sperm whale puts things in a different perspective for her.

Lester, Helen. *Three Cheers for Tacky.* Houghton Mifflin, 1994. Tacky the Penguin adds his own unique touch to his team's routine at the Penguin Cheering Contest. Also: *Tacky the Penguin.*

Pfister, Marcus. *Penguin Pete and Little Tim.* North-South, 1994. While taking a walk with his father, a little penguin throws snowballs, rides a dogsled, slides down a slippery slope, and swims with seals.

Woods, Audrey. *Little Penguin's Tale.* Harcourt Brace Jovanovich, 1989. Looking for fun, little Penguin dances with gooney birds, plays at the Walrus Polar Club, and narrowly escapes being eaten by a whale.

Penguin

After your penguin stories, allow the children to make a paper penguin. This craft takes ten minutes to complete, if all the parts are precut. You may want to have parents or other adult helpers assist with this craft.

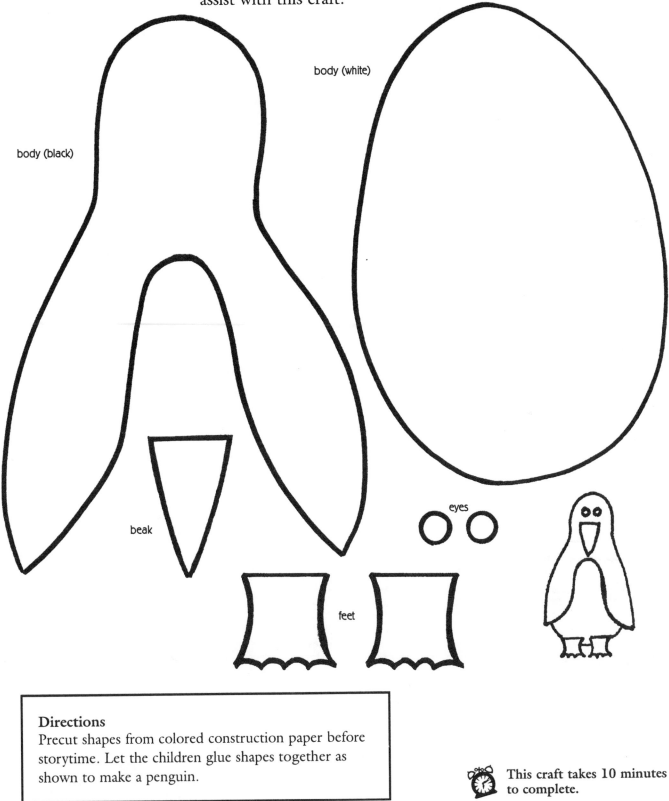

body (white)

body (black)

beak

eyes

feet

Directions
Precut shapes from colored construction paper before storytime. Let the children glue shapes together as shown to make a penguin.

This craft takes **10 minutes** to complete.

Pigs

Before Sharing Books

If you're adventurous, wear a pig snout to storytime. Say, "Hi. I'm a pig. Pigs eat lots of corn and grain. We soon grow big and fat. Our most important job is supplying the farmer with bacon. We are very clean animals, but you may see us rolling in the mud to stay cool. Our noses are called snouts." Invite the children to be pigs for a day! Explain the benefits, such as cooling off in a mud puddle and having lots of kitchen scraps to eat. Lead them in a pig cheer (which is a grunt). Then tape a pig snout on each child.

Rest Activities

Fingerplays and Action Rhymes

This Little Pig

This little pig went to market. *(touch thumb and wiggle it)*

This little pig went home. *(touch index finger and wiggle it)*

This little pig had roast beef. *(touch middle finger and wiggle it)*

This little pig had none. *(touch ring finger and wiggle it)*

This little pig cried "Wee, wee, wee," all the way home. *(touch little finger and wiggle it)*

This may also be done on the toes!
[Traditional]

Piggy in the Barn

Piggy, piggy in the barn, *(put tips of fingers together to form a roof)*

Don't come out just yet! *(shake finger)*

It's raining hard, and don't forget, *(wiggle fingers from high to low, like raindrops)*

Your curly tail might straighten out, *(curl index finger—then straighten it)*

If you get it wet!

Tom Tom, the Piper's Son

Tom Tom, the Piper's son.

Stole a pig and away he run. *(grabbing motion, then make a fist & run in place)*

The pig got eat. *(put fist to mouth and pretend to eat)*

And Tom got beat. *(clap hands)*

And he went crying down the street. *(run in place very fast)*
[Traditional]

Books to Share

Alarcon, Karen Beaumont. *Luella Mae, She's Run Away*. Henry Holt, 1997. A growing crowd searches for the missing Luella Mae, a pig.

Galdone, Paul. *The Amazing Pig: An Old Hungarian Tale*. Houghton Mifflin, 1981. The king believes almost all of the tales a farm boy tells about his wonderful pig.

Hutchins, Pat. *Little Pink Pig*. Greenwillow, 1994. When it is time for bed, a little pink pig lags behind as his mother asks the horse, cow, sheep and hens to help her find her child.

McNaughton, Collin. *Suddenly*. Harcourt Brace, 1995. Time after time, Preston the pig unknowingly outwits a hungry wolf that is trying to catch him and eat him.

Pomerantz, Charlotte. *The Piggy in the Puddle*. Macmillan, 1974. Unable to keep a young pig from frolicking in the mud, her family finally joins her for a mud party.

Waddell, Martin. *The Pig in the Pond*. Candlewick, 1992. An overheated pig who doesn't swim, throws himself into a pond, throwing the farmyard into an uproar.

Wilhelm, Hans. *Oh, What a Mess*. Crown, 1988. After Franklin Pig wins first prize in an art contest, his very messy family begins to put their home in order.

Pig Puppet on a Paper Bag

As part of your storytime, you may help each child make a paper bag puppet. Or, you can give each child a fingerpuppet to wear.

Bag puppet mouth

Bag puppet head

Directions for Bag Puppet
Copy and cut out the pattern for each child before storytime. Allow the children to color the pig face. Then help them glue the face and mouth to a small brown paper bag as shown. Glue sticks work well and dry quickly.

Pig Snout
Tape snout to children before reading the pig stories.

Directions for Finger Puppet
Copy and cut out a puppet for each child. Tape before storytime.

Paper Bag Puppet takes 10 minutes to complete if all parts are precut.

Rabbits

Before Sharing Books

A real bunny will be a great attention getter for this storytime, but a toy or puppet will work just as well. Spend some time talking about the anatomy of a rabbit. Ask the children if they can guess why rabbits are so fast.

Rest Activities

Fingerplays and Action Rhymes

Many cute poems can be found in:
Bunnies, Bunnies, Bunnies: A Treasury of Stories, Songs and Poems by Walter Retan. Silver Press, 1991.

This Is the Bunny

This is the bunny with ears so funny. *(fist with two fingers raised)*

This is the hole in the ground. *(cup other hand)*

When a noise he hears, he pricks up his ears,

And jumps into the ground. *(fist dives into cupped hand)*

[Traditional]

Song

In a Cottage in the Wood

In a cottage in the wood,
Little man by the window stood.

Saw a rabbit running by,
Knocking at the door.

"Help me. Help me. Help me," he said.
"Or the hunter will shoot me dead."

"Come, little rabbit, come with me.
Happy we will be."

[Traditional]

Books to Share

Arnosky, Jim. *Rabbits and Raindrops.* Putnam, 1997. Mother rabbit's five babies hop out of her nest to nibble clover, meet grasshoppers, spiders and bees, and run for shelter when it rains.

Baron, Alan. *Red Fox and the Baby Bunnies.* Candlewick, 1997. Dan Dog and Tabby Cat rescue the baby bunnies from hungry Red Fox in a most unexpected way.

Dodds, Dayle Ann. *Do Bunnies Talk?* HarperCollins, 1992. Introduces sounds made by animals, humans and machines, but not bunnies because they never speak. Or do they?

Karlin, Nurit. *Ten Little Bunnies.* Simon & Schuster, 1994. Rhyming text describes how various mishaps reduce ten little bunnies down to one.

Lowell, Susan. *The Tortoise and the Jackrabbit.* Northland, 1994. Many of the animals that live in the southwest witness the race between slow but steady Tortoise and quick, overconfident Jackrabbit.

Maris, Ron. *Runaway Rabbit.* Delacorte, 1989. A runaway pet rabbit encounters dogs, a duck and other animals before being recaptured.

Shannon, George. *Dance Away.* Greenwillow, 1982. Rabbit's dancing saves his friends from becoming Fox's supper.

Rabbit Puzzle

Finish up your rabbit storytime by allowing the children to put together a rabbit puzzle.

Directions

Copy the rabbit picture for each child. Cut it out and then cut the rabbit into three or four pieces. Paper clip the pieces together or put them into a small bag for each child. Let the children arrange on a piece of construction paper, glue in place and color.

This craft takes **10 minutes** to complete.

Snakes

Before Sharing Books

Invite someone to story time that has a real snake. Let the children touch the snake. Ask them to describe how the snake feels. Is it cold? Is it slimy? Is it fuzzy? Is it smooth? Ask them to describe how the snake looks. Is it colorful? Is it beautiful? Is it big?

Rest Activities

Fingerplays and Action Rhymes

The Snake and the Dog

One little snake was basking in the sun. *(hold up one finger)*

Along came a dog looking for some fun. *(hands up like paws, pant like a dog)*

"*Hiss, hiss,*" went the snake. *(make a hissing noise, make hand wiggle like a snake)*

"*Bow wow,*" barked the dog. *(barking noise, paws up and pant like a dog)*

Whoosh! went the snake into a hollow log. *(make hand wiggle quickly away)*

I Am a Snake!

I have no legs. I have no arms. *(arms down, close to body)*

I can take off my skin. *(pretend to pull of skin)*

I wiggle my tongue like this. *(wiggle tongue)*

I'm very, very thin. *(hands on ribs, slide them down)*

I can open my mouth so wide, *(open mouth)*

And eat my dinner whole! *(rub tummy)*

I can curl up nice and tight, *(squat down low)*

Or stretch out like a pole! *(stretch up tall)*

Poem

"I'm Being Eaten By a Boa Constrictor" from *Where the Sidewalk Ends* by Shel Silverstein.

Books to Share

Ayliffe, Alex. *Slither, Swoop, Swing.* Viking, 1993. Shows different ways that snakes, bats, monkeys and other animals move.

Baker, Keith. *Hide and Snake.* Harcourt Brace Jovanovich, 1991. A brightly colored snake challenges readers to a game of hide and seek as he hides among familiar objects.

Gray, Libba Moore. *Small Green Snake.* Orchard, 1994. Despite mother's warning not to wander, Small Green Snake wiggles away to investigate the new sound from across the garden wall.

Hall, Kirsten. *I'm Not Scared.* Children's Press, 1994. Two boys who are not afraid of heights, bees or snakes need some reassurance when they hear noises while camping at night.

McNulty, Faith. *A Snake in the House.* Scholastic, 1994. An escaped snake finds many clever places to hide throughout the house, while the boy who brought him home continues to search for him.

Noble, Trinka Hakes. *The Day Jimmy's Boa Ate the Wash.* Dial, 1980. Jimmy's boa constrictor wreaks havoc on the class trip to the farm.

Shannon, George. *April Showers.* Greenwillow, 1995. A group of frogs enjoys dancing in the rain so much that they seem not to notice a snake sneaking up on them.

Slotboom, Wendy. *King Snake.* Houghton Mifflin, 1997. A talkative snake captures two mice, but his verbosity helps them escape.

Walsh, Ellen Stohl. *Mouse Count.* Harcourt Brace Jovanovich, 1991. Ten mice outsmart a hungry snake.

Snake Puppet

After your storytime help the children make a snake puppet.

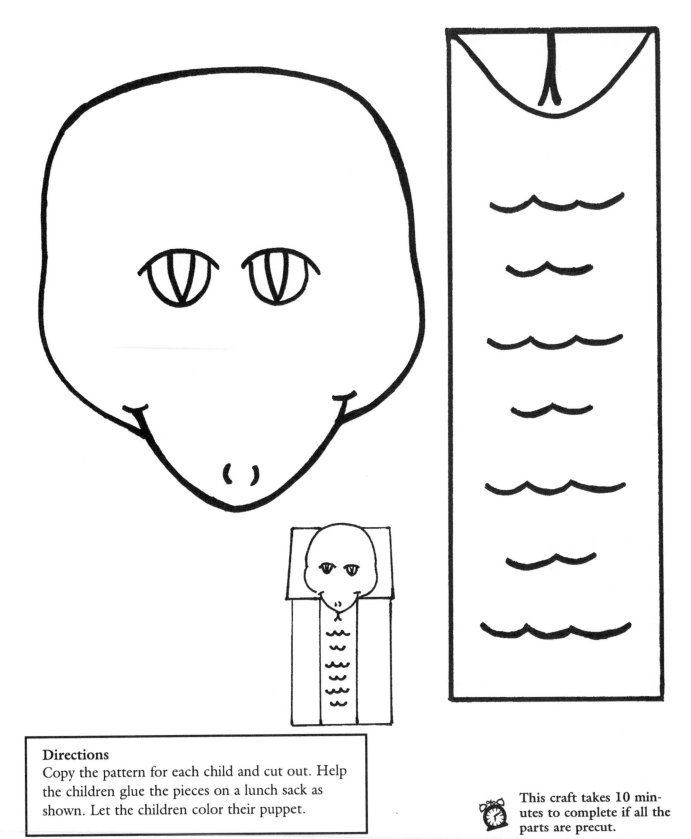

Directions
Copy the pattern for each child and cut out. Help the children glue the pieces on a lunch sack as shown. Let the children color their puppet.

This craft takes 10 minutes to complete if all the parts are precut.

Snow

Before Sharing Books

Bring snow globes to storytime. Shake them and ask the children about what is falling in the globe. Ask them if it snows in the summer or the winter. If you have snow in your area, bring some to storytime and make a snowball to pass around the room. Have everyone put on their pretend mittens and hat, so they can stay warm as you read the snow stories.

Rest Activities

Songs

Ten Little Snowmen
"Tune of: 10 Little Indians"

One little, two little, three little snowmen.
Four little, five little, six little snowmen.
Seven little, eight little, nine little snowmen.
Ten little snowmen tall.

Ten little, nine little, eight little snowmen,
Seven little, six little, five little snowmen,
Four little, three little, two little snowmen,
One little snowman small.

Extend fingers as you count up. Fold one under as you count down.

I'm a Little Snowman
Tune of: "I'm a Little Teapot"
I'm a little snowman,
Short and fat.
Here is my broom, *(pretend to hold broom handle)*
and here is my hat. *(touch head)*
When it's cold and icy,
I will stay.
When it's hot,
I will melt away. *(shrink down to the floor)*

Where Is Snowman
Tune of: "Where Is Thumbkin"
Where is snowman? Where is snowman?
Here I am. Here I am. *(hold up each index finger)*
How are you today, sir?
Very well, I thank you. *(wiggle each index finger as if talking)*
Melt away. Melt away. *(fold index finger into the fist)*

Books to Share

Armstrong, Jennifer. *The Snowball.* Random House, 1996. A small snowball gets bumped by a skier and rolls down the hill growing in size and picking up people as it goes.

Brenner, Barbara. *The Snow Parade.* Crown, 1984. An increasing number of animals and people join Andrew in his parade through the snow.

Christelow, Eileen. *The Five-Dog Night.* Clarion, 1993. Old Betty tries to give her neighbor Ezra advice on how to survive the cold winter nights.

Florian, Douglas. *A Winter Day.* Greenwillow, 1987. A family enjoys a winter day of relaxation and fun.

Galbraith, Kathryn. *Look! Snow!* McElderry, 1992. The first snow of the season brings great enjoyment to the town's human and animal inhabitants.

Inkpen, Mick. *Kipper's Snowy Day.* Harcourt Brace, 1996. Kipper the dog spends the day enjoying the snow with his best friend, Tiger.

Lewis, Kim. *First Snow.* Candlewick, 1993. On a trip up the hill with her mother to feed the sheep, a young girl loses her teddy bear when it starts snowing.

Shade, Susan. *Snow Bugs.* Random House, 1997. The snow bugs discover wonderful ways to play on a snowy day.

Snowman Straw

Finish up your snowy stories by helping the children make snowman straws. This craft takes five minutes if the parts are precut. You may wish to serve a small cup of juice and allow the children to sip it through their straws.

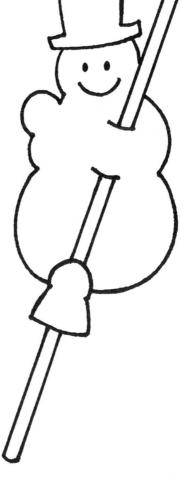

Directions

Before storytime, cut snowman out of white paper, cut hat out of black paper and cut broom out of yellow paper. Cut slits in the snowman for the drinking straw. Let children draw features on the face and paste the hat on the snowman. Insert the straw through the slits, then let children paste the broom on the straw.

 This craft takes 5 minutes to complete if the parts are all precut.

Spiders

Before Sharing Books

Lead the children in the following creative dramatic scene:

Let's pretend we are birds and we are flying high above the trees, the houses, the streets, the parks, and the stores. Now we are going to fly lower, because we are looking for food. We want to eat some nice beetles, or worms. Let's fly down to a tree and sit on a branch. From there we can look for something good to eat. From our branch on the tree, we can see something shiny, and lacey and beautiful. It is a spider web that has been hung between the tiny branches of this tree. In the middle of the web, we see a pretty spider. "Hello, Spider," we say. "I see you are also hoping to catch something good to eat." The spider answers, "Yes. I am waiting for an insect to get caught in my web. Would you like to hear a story while we wait? I really like to tell stories." So we settle down on our branch of the tree to hear the spider's stories.

Rest Activities

Fingerplays and Action Rhymes

Little Miss Muffet

Little Miss Muffet,
Sat on a tuffet,
Eating her curds and whey.
Along came a spider,
And sat down beside her,
And frightened Miss Muffet away.

Try using creative dramatics to act out this poem.

Wiggle Waggle Like a Spider

My arms go *UP*,
Or *DOWN* instead.
My arms go *ROUND AND ROUND* the web.
My fingers go *SNAP*,
My toes go *TAP*,
My body goes *WIGGLE WAGGLE*,
Just like that. *(clap)*

Fist time, speak in normal voice while doing the actions. Second time, speak a little softer. Third time, whisper. Fourth time, do only the actions.

Books to Share

Kimmel, Eric. ***Anansi and the Talking Melon.*** Holiday House, 1994. A clever spider tricks Elephant and some other animals into thinking the melon in which he is hiding can talk.

Kirk, David. ***Miss Spider's Wedding.*** Scholastic, 1995. Miss Spider proves that her heart knows best when it comes to choosing a husband. Also: *Miss Spider's Tea Party*

Oppenheim, Joanne. ***Eency Weency Spider.*** Gareth Stevens, 1997. After climbing the water spout, Eency Weency Spider meets Little Miss Muffet, Humpty Dumpty and Little Jack Horner.

Raffi. ***Spider on the Floor.*** Crown, 1993. Illustrated text to the song about the curious spider.

Sardegna, Jill. ***The Roly Poly Spider.*** Scholastic, 1994. After eating a beetle, a caterpillar, a bumblebee and other insects, a plump spider gets stuck in a waterspout.

Simon, Francesca. ***Spider School.*** Dial, 1996. Because Kate got out on the wrong side of the bed, her first day at a new school proves to be a real nightmare, with a gorilla for a teacher and spiders for lunch.

Temple, Frances. ***Tiger Soup: An Anansi Story from Jamaica.*** Orchard, 1994. Anansi tricks tiger into leaving the soup he has been cooking.

Van Laan, Nancy. ***This Is the Hat.*** Jay Street Books, 1992. Cumulative verses follow an old man's hat as it becomes a home for a spider, a mouse, and other creatures.

Spider

Finish up your spider storytime by helping the children make a paper spider. You may then use the spider to act out the song, "Spider on the Floor." If your storytime kids are ages two or three, you may want to invite parents to assist them with gluing.

leg

body

Directions

Copy one body and four legs for each child on black paper and cut out before storytime. Let the children curl the body into a cylinder and glue or staple it. Let the children glue the legs to the bottom of the body as shown. Curl or bend the legs down. Use small circle labels to add eyes and a nose to the spider body. Attach a 15" piece of yarn or string to the body for hanging the spider.

 This craft takes 10 minutes to complete.

Spring

Before Sharing Books

Collect some items that remind you of spring, such as an umbrella, a packet of flower seeds, some baby animal pictures or toys, a kite or wind sock. Play a guessing game with the children, saying "I am thinking of something wet and small that makes things grow. I am thinking of something tiny and yellow that comes from an egg." After they have guessed all of your items, see if they know what season these things remind you of.

Rest Activities

Fingerplays and Action Rhymes

My Garden

I dig, dig, dig, *(digging motions)*

And plant some seeds. *(poke finger between fingers of other hand)*

I rake, rake, rake, *(raking motions)*

And pull some weeds. *(pull upward with fingers from palm of hand)*

I wait and watch. *(hands on hips)*

And soon I know, *(point to head)*

My garden will sprout, *hands low, palms down)*

And start to grow! *(raise hands toward ceiling)*

Songs

Caterpillar Song

(Tune: Frere Jacques)

Caterpillar, caterpillar,

In the tree, in the tree.

First you wiggle this way,

Then you wiggle that way.

Look at me! Look at me!

Spring Song

Tune of: "Good Night, Ladies"

Drip and drizzle. Drip and drizzle. Drip and drizzle.

I'll put on my boots. *(make raindrops with fingers, pull on boots)*

Brr, it's freezing. Brr, it's freezing. Brr, it's freezing.

I'll zip up my coat. *(hug body, zip coat)*

Whoosh ! Wind blowing. Whoosh! Wind blowing. Whoosh! Wind blowing.

I'll put on my hat. *(wave hands above head, put hands on head)*

Sun is shining. Sun is shining. Sun is shining.

Go outside and play. Hey! *(arms in circle over head, jump)*

Books to Share

Baxter, Nicola. *Spring.* Children's Press, 1996. A simple discussion about changes in the weather, planting gardens, and the birth of baby animals.

Dabcovich, Lydia. *Sleepy Bear.* Dutton, 1982. A bear gets ready for his long winter nap and then awakens again in the spring.

Fleming, Denise. *In the Small, Small Pond.* Holt, 1993. Rhyming text describes the activities of animals living in and near a pond as spring progresses into fall.

Hoban, Lillian. *Arthur's Camp-Out.* HarperCollins, 1993. Arthur goes on an overnight field trip in the woods behind his house during spring vacation.

Hutchins, Pat. *The Wind Blew.* MacMillan, 1974; Aladdin Paperbacks, 1993. A rhymed tale describing the antics of a capricious wind.

Kinsey-Warnock, Natalie. *When Spring Comes.* Dutton, 1993. A child living on a farm in the early 1900s, describes some of the activities that mark the approach of spring.

Pacovska, Kveta. *The Little Flower King.* North-South, 1996. A lonely king searches for a princess to marry and finds one within one of his beloved tulips.

Serfozo, Mary. *Rain Talk.* McElderry, 1990. A child enjoys a glorious day in the rain, listening to the varied sounds it makes as it falls.

Growing Tulip

Help the children make a tulip that grows.

Directions
Copy tulip pattern on colored paper and cut out. Cut a slit in the bottom of a plain white paper cup for each child. Let the children glue a craft stick onto their tulip. Insert the craft stick in the slit in the paper cup. Push the stick up and the tulip grows. If time allows, children may color the tulip and draw grass on the paper cup with markers.

This craft takes 5 minutes to complete.

Stars

Before Sharing Books

Hang paper stars around your storytime room and suspend some from the ceiling. Tell the children that you are going to wish. Recite the wishing poem with them, and then ask them what they would wish for on the first star of the evening. As a group, wish for some star stories. Then pull out your first book and begin.

Rest Activities

Fingerplays and Action Rhymes

Blast Off! Poems About Space by Lee Bennett Hopkins. HarperCollins, 1995. A collection of poems about the moon, stars, planets and astronauts.

Day and Night

Moon comes out. *(hold hand out to form a crescent)*

Sun goes in. *(place other hand behind back)*

Here is a blanket to cuddle your chin. *(place hands under chin)*

Moon goes in. *(place moon hand behind back)*

And Sun comes out. *(hold hand out with fingers extended like sun rays)*

Throw off the blankets and bustle about! *(fling arms out wide and wiggle body)*

[Traditional]

Sally Go Round the Sun

Sally go round the sun,
Sally go round the moon,
Sally go round the stars,
Every afternoon.

Hold hands, walk in a circle. All sit down on the word "afternoon."
[Traditional]

Song

Twinkle, Twinkle Little Star

Twinkle, twinkle little star.
How I wonder what you are.
Up above the world so high,
Like a diamond in the sky.
Twinkle, twinkle little star.
How I wonder what you are.
[Traditional song]

Books to Share

Asimov, Isaac. *Why Do Stars Twinkle?* Gareth Stevens, 1991. This book explains why stars in the night sky appear to twinkle.

Boyd, Lizi. *Sweet Dreams, Willy.* Viking, 1992. Not wanting to sleep at bedtime, Willy goes in search of others still awake, and has an adventure in the night world of birds, fish, the moon and the stars.

Field, Susan. *The Sun, the Moon, and the Silver Baboon.* HarperCollins, 1993. A baboon rescues a star that is caught in a tree.

Hong, Lilly Toy. *How the Ox Star Fell From Heaven.* Whitman, 1991. A Chinese folktale which explains

why the ox was banished from heaven to become the farmer's beast of burden.

Talor, Jane. *Twinkle, Twinkle Little Star.* Morrow, 1992. The familiar children's poem is illustrated by Michael Hague.

Taylor, Harriet Peck. *Coyote Places the Stars.* Bradbury, 1993. Coyote arranges the stars in the shapes of his animals friends in this legend from the Wasco Indians.

Young, Ruth. *Golden Bear.* Viking, 1992. Golden Bear and his friend learn to do many things, including wishing on stars.

Star Pasta Necklace

Finish up your star stories by making your choice of two crafts, either a star pasta necklace or a glow in the dark light switch cover. You may wish to invite parents to help with this craft.

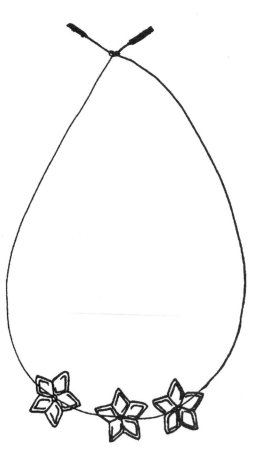

Directions
Cut yarn or string into 18" lengths, one for each child. Wrap the ends of the string with masking tape to make them stiff. Buy star-shaped dry pasta. Help the children push the string through the pasta. When they have put several pieces on the string, tie the ends together to make a necklace.

 This craft takes 5 minutes to complete.

Glowing Light Switch Cover

Directions
Buy a plastic light switch cover for each child. Copy the design on stiff paper and cut out, using an Exacto knife to cut out the center and punch holes for the screws. Glue the design to the light switch cover before storytime. Let the children color the design with markers. Trace the stars with glow-in-the-dark tube paint. Let the paint dry. If desired, cover the switch cover with clear contact paper after the paint is dry.

 This craft takes 10 minutes to complete.

Zoo

Before Sharing Books

Bring an assortment of zoo animal toys or puppets to display with your books. Tell the children you are going for a walk to a fun place. As you walk around the room, give them hints about where you are going. This place is noisy. It is a good place to take a picnic lunch. This place has big animals and small animals. When you arrive at your "zoo," you may want to have the children make various loud animal noises, and then have them make the sound of a giraffe, which is very quiet.

Rest Activities

Fingerplays and Action Rhymes

Five Little Monkeys

Five little monkeys, *(hold up five fingers)*
Swinging in a tree. *(swing hands over head)*
Teasing Mr. Crocodile, *(shake one finger)*
You can't catch me.
You can't catch me. *(point to self, shake head)*

Up comes Mr. Crocodile, quiet as can be.
 (palms together, move hands forward)
Snap! *(clap hands sharply)*

Repeat with four, three, two and one.

Songs

Alice the Camel

Alice the camel has three humps,
Alice the camel has three humps.
Go Alice Go!
Bump. Bump. Bump.

*Stand in a circle with arms around each other,
When you say bump, bump hips. Repeat with 2
humps, 1 hump. Last verse, pretend to cry.*

Alice the Camel has no humps.
Because Alice is a horse!

Pop! Goes the Weasel

All around the cobbler's bench, *(turn in a circle)*
The monkey chased the weasel. *(make grabbing motions)*
The monkey thought it was all in fun, *(shake one finger)*
Pop! Goes the weasel. *(clap hands)*

Books to Share

Carlstrom, Nancy. *What Would You Do If You Lived at the Zoo?* Little, Brown, 1994. Animal noises and actions are the answers to questions posed in rhyme.

Denim, Sue. *The Dumb Bunnies Go to the Zoo.* Blue Sky, 1997. When the Dumb Bunnies visit the zoo they let all of the animals out of their cages because they mistake a butterfly for an escaped lion.

Ford, Miela. *Follow the Leader.* Greenwillow, 1996. Two polar bears at the zoo play follow-the-leader.

Fox, Mem. *Zoo-Looking.* Mondo, 1996. While Flora visits the zoo with her father, not only does she look at the animals but some of them turn to look at her.

Hendrick, Mary Jean. *If Anything Ever Goes Wrong at the Zoo.* Harcourt Brace Jovanovich, 1993. A young girl and her family get some unusual houseguests after a series of zoo emergencies have zookeepers looking for temporary housing for the animals.

Hoban, Tana. *A Children's Zoo.* Greenwillow, 1985. Color photographs of animals are accompanied by several descriptive words.

Paxton, Tom. *Going to the Zoo.* Morrow, 1996. Enthusiastic siblings describe the animals at the zoo. The text is a children's song.

Rice, Eve. *Sam, Who Never Forgets.* Greenwillow, 1977. A zookeeper almost forgets to feed the animals.

Roaring Big Cat

Make your zoo storytime a roaring success by helping the children make a Roaring Big Cat! Adult help may be required for two and three year olds.

Directions

Copy and cut out the face, mouth, tongue and nose before storytime. Then follow numbered directions for assembly.

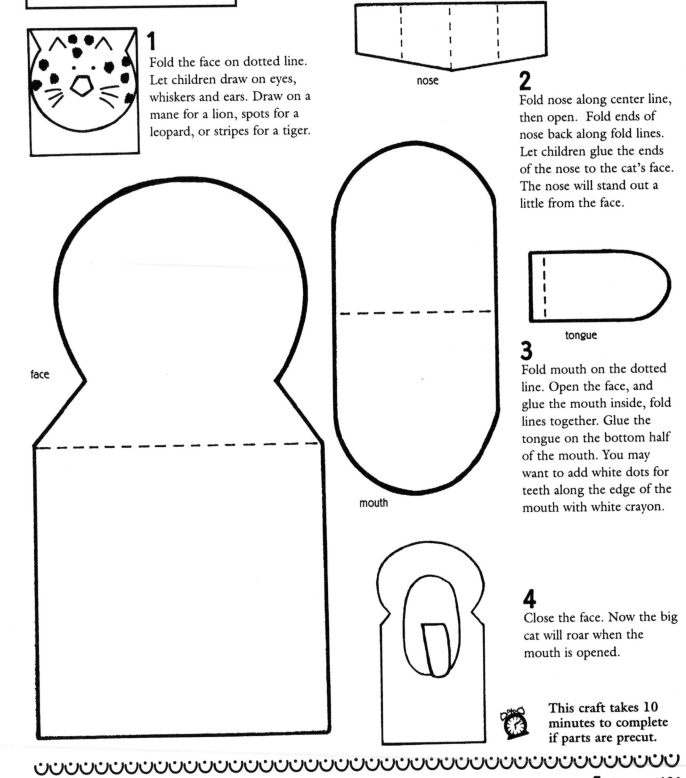

1 Fold the face on dotted line. Let children draw on eyes, whiskers and ears. Draw on a mane for a lion, spots for a leopard, or stripes for a tiger.

nose

2 Fold nose along center line, then open. Fold ends of nose back along fold lines. Let children glue the ends of the nose to the cat's face. The nose will stand out a little from the face.

tongue

3 Fold mouth on the dotted line. Open the face, and glue the mouth inside, fold lines together. Glue the tongue on the bottom half of the mouth. You may want to add white dots for teeth along the edge of the mouth with white crayon.

face

mouth

4 Close the face. Now the big cat will roar when the mouth is opened.

This craft takes **10 minutes** to complete if parts are precut.